Tenino Washington

The Decades of Boom & Bust

by
Scott McArthur

First Edition

ISBN: 0-9772954-0-0
Library of Congress Control Number : 2005908438

About the cover: The original Tenino railroad depot,
with wood-burning locomotive and passenger train, about 1885.
(University of Washington Special Collections, Neg. No. UW23984.)

Published by Scott McArthur
P. O. Box 368
Monmouth, OR 97361

Printed in the United States of America

Contents

FOREWORD

Why bother to write the history of a small town like Tenino? There is no profit in it. The market for small books like this is really quite small. That's why we local history authors have to pay to publish our own works. But local history is the ultimate history. It tells how people lived, what they did and why they did what they did. Local history tells the story that professional historians do not. To paraphrase the explanation of author Tony Horowitz: We are the keepers of the past, like those monks with their Latin books back in the Dark Ages. We keep the true story alive. Some day, centuries from now, when folks come looking for history, we can say, "Here it is. We kept it for you."

ABOUT THIS BOOK:

I have checked and double-checked the material in this book for accuracy. But I know there may be errors, and if so, I apologize. Let me know if you find something you think is wrong. I'll check it out and fix it for the next printing.

Scott McArthur
P.O. Box 368
Monmouth, OR 97361

INTRODUCTION

This book took decades to materialize. My father was Robert R. McArthur (1900-1984). His father was William McArthur (1866-1940), a leader in the Tenino sandstone industry of the period.

I was born in Olympia and raised in Tacoma. Dad was a great storyteller. When I was a kid he told me stories of his boyhood in Tenino. Maybe it was because I was an only child, and he told tales of a family with four lively youngsters in it. Maybe it was because the early days of Tenino seemed romantic to a kid being raised in the city with a population of 100,000.

I remembered those stories. I visited in Tenino each summer with my aunt, Bernice McArthur Mandery, her husband, Avard, a one-time football star at the University of Nebraska, and their three kids, Lee Ann, Beverly and Duane. We had a great time during those visits.

When something came in print about Tenino, I saved it. The earliest clipping in my file is from the Tacoma News-Tribune of October 24, 1943. That article authenticated and gave more detail to Dad's story of Indian Louie Quityamals and William McArthur's Edison talking machine. (See Chapter 16.)

Another link to the past was the family's collection of photographs. William McArthur liked pictures of things. On special occasions such as holidays and civic events he would hire a commercial photographer from Centralia who would haul his huge camera, tripod and a can of flash powder by train to Tenino. There he photographed the event at my grandfather's direction. Those photos were printed, mounted on gray cardboard and wound up in a trunk in the back bedroom closet of my grandmother's house. I have many of these. Others are elsewhere in the family.

I moved to Oregon from Tacoma in 1955. But my fascination with Tenino never ceased.

In 1980, my folks came down to visit us. Dad was in poor health. I determined to collect his story and his memories.

I pulled out the tape recorder one afternoon, placed it on the dining room table, turned it on and declared that he was about to be a part of oral history.

I asked questions. Dad didn't answer. "Why won't you answer?" I inquired. "I may not remember it right," he responded.

So I let it drop until the next evening after dinner when, without the tape recorder, I started to query him again. This time he answered. And every 10 minutes or so I would excuse myself, retreat to the bathroom, close the door, jot down the answers on a note pad I had stashed in the towel cabinet, flush the toilet and go back out to the living room to renew the questions. I am sure Dad must have been suspicious. Or maybe he just thought I had a problem with my personal plumbing.

But he told his story. And I had it written down.

After Dad died, my mother, Beatrice Norton McArthur, brought forth a notebook in which she had written the stories he had told her over the years about Tenino. She had taught in the grade school there in the 1920s and that was how they met.

I combined the two of those, added some of Dad's recollections that had otherwise bubbled to the surface of my memory, and put together a talk which I gave to the South Thurston County Historical Society in 1995.

They had a good crowd that day. I promised Jean Montgomery, then the president and still a stalwart of the Society, that I would write a book some day.

Well, here it is. I have fleshed out Dad's stories from other historical sources. I particularly am grateful for the excellent research work of David A. Knoblach, a geologist of Milton, Washington, who is the expert on the history of the stone quarry industry in Washington State.

All of Tenino is indebted to Don Major, for 40 years the editor and publisher of the Thurston County (later Tenino) Independent. Don Major had the interest and good sense to publish over a six month period in 1935 interviews with many of the Tenino's early residents then surviving.

Also to be credited is Art Dwelley, Major's successor as editor and publisher of the Independent, who wrote extensively about Tenino's heritage, including his book: "Prairies & Quarries; Pioneer Days Around Tenino, 1830-1900." Art intended to do a follow-up book on Tenino's history after 1900, but he never got it written.

William McArthur's partner was Hans P. Scheel. In 1995, Sally Larsen Phillips, H. P. Scheel's granddaughter, wrote the memories of her mother, Margaret Scheel Larsen. I have quoted several times from her excellent account. Sally, her husband Keith Phillips, her mother and David Scheel, another of H. P. Scheel's grandchildren, also reviewed my first draft and offered valuable suggestions. And of course, my McArthur cousins, Lee Ann Mandery, Beverly McCormack, Duane Mandery, Joanie Guggenmos, Penny Burkhalter and Norine Tibbits. These folks, the dearest friends of my childhood, kindly reviewed my first draft and offered suggestions and corrections.

A great help was that of Norman Montgomery of the South Thurston County Historical Society, who opened up the museum on days when it was closed and helped me go through the Society's marvelous collection of photographs.

This book covers the period from 1888, when the first stone quarry opened, through the 1930s, when the local bank failed for the second time and the last of the quarries closed for good. The period includes the years that my Dad spent in Tenino. He came with his family to Tenino in 1903 and left in 1927 to work for the L. E. Titus Ford dealership in Olympia. There is some overlap in time intended to put things into context.

In my writing, I refer frequently to "Dad". That's my father, Robert R. McArthur.

You may have a little trouble keeping the McArthurs straight. In those days there were in Tenino three William McArthurs, three Robert McArthurs and two Andrew McArthurs. It was the custom in this branch of the McArthurs to name the first three male children Robert, William and Andrew, in no particular order. (That practice is a good way to confuse history.) Thus my grandfather, William McArthur, and his two brothers, Andrew and Robert. That rule was followed in my dad's family, too. Dad's brother William Dewey McArthur was the first to be born. Dad, Robert R. McArthur, was the second. The third son was supposed to be named Andrew. But my Grandmother, Margaret Beattie McArthur, didn't like the name Andrew. Granddad William McArthur was out of town on business when this new baby was born. When he got home he found that Grandma had already named the baby and had him baptized as Teddie McArthur—named after Theodore Roosevelt, the president at the time.

Oh, to finish the family account: My Dad, Robert R.

McArthur, became the sales manager for L. E. Titus' chain of Ford dealerships. The Titus company went broke in 1932 and so did Dad. He wound up owning a Tidewater Associated service station in Tacoma, where I learned to work. ("You run, you do not walk to the pump island," my father taught me. "You wash the glass all around the car and you keep the rest rooms clean.") Dad died in 1984 at the age of 84.

1

TENINO'S GOLDEN YEARS

Tenino started out as a hotel and store at the end of the railroad track.

Then it expanded as a transfer point between two railroads, and later as a trading center for the farming and lumbering community that surrounded it.

Growth began in the late 1880s with the opening of Tenino's first two stone quarries.

But the real boom began with the establishment in 1903 of the Hercules Sandstone Co.'s Quarry No. 1 west of town and the start of commercial coal mining activities south of town.

In 1907 the R. L. Polk Co.'s commercial index of Washington and Oregon showed Tenino had a population of 300.

By 1915, the Hercules Sandstone Co. employed as many as 400 men in its area stone quarries. The competitor Tenino Stone Company continued in operation at the south edge of town. Several saw mills were in operation. Speculators drilled for the oil they knew lay (but never could find) under the Tenino country. The town was incorporated. It was becoming a lively place with as many as 11 saloons. A full panoply of commercial establishments lined the main street. The 1915 R. L. Polk directory showed a population of 1,053.

Tenino even survived the collapse of its only bank and the bankruptcy of its largest sawmill.

The Tenino State Bank was organized in 1906. W. Dean Hayes, an experienced banker, was brought in to run it.

Hayes did a bang-up job of it. The bank served the community well and Hays became a leader of the community and represented Thurston County in the 1913 state legislature.

Hayes left the Tenino State Bank in August 1914 to organize the Olympia Bank and Trust Company.

Both the Tenino State Bank and Hays' new bank at Olympia were solidly based. But Hays made one fatal mistake. He arranged for the surplus cash of both banks to be held – at interest – by the United States National Bank of Centralia. The Centralia bank was a federal bank and a logical place for smaller state banks to deposit their surplus cash, a common practice before the Federal Reserve banks that hold bank deposits today.

The United States National Bank of Centralia and its satellite Union Loan and Trust Company were run by Charles Gilchrist. Gilchrist was a banker of considerable reputation. The bank was insolvent, however, and Gilchrist, it was discovered, had stolen from his own bank.

The Centralia banks failed. Down with them went the Tenino State Bank and the Olympia Bank and Trust Company.

Thurston County Prosecuting Attorney Thomas L. O'Leary, in the final months of his term of office, brought a blizzard of criminal charges against Hays and against Isaac Blumauer, president of the Tenino bank. Each was charged with multiple charges of larceny. These were technical charges involving transfers of funds during the final days before the banks closed.

Hays went on trial in the Thurston County Superior Court in

December. The trial lasted a week. It took the jury seven minutes to deliberate and return a verdict of not guilty. Blumauer's trial jury took 25 minutes to acquit him.

Gilchrist had been convicted of federal charges of embezzlement and was serving a five year sentence in the McNeil Island federal prison. Gilchrist was brought back to Olympia to testify in both trials.

Both Hays and Blumauer were ruined as a result. Hays, considered a shoe-in for reelection to the Legislature, was forced to withdraw from the race.

Blumauer's two companies, the Blumauer Logging Company and the Blumauer Timber Company, went into bankruptcy.

In February 1915 the 11 shareholders of the failed Tenino State Bank were assessed by the Superior Court receiver to help make up the depositors' losses. Hays had to pay $5,100, Blumauer $1,100 and the other shareholders $100 to $1,100 each.

Depositors in the Tenino Bank eventually recovered 50 cents on the dollar from their deposits.

Tenino's quarry industry collapsed before the start of World War I. The big Grays Harbor jetty project that brought the opening of the Hercules Company's No. 6 quarry up the Skookumchuck River was cancelled. Modern brick, steel and concrete building techniques ended the widespread use of cut stone as a primary building material.

But the booming timber industry kept payrolls in the area and farming activities supported the Tenino business community through the 1920s.

Then, on the heels of the stock market crash of 1929 came the Great Depression.

Tenino hit the bottom.

The Citizen's Bank of Tenino, which was organized in 1914

after the Tenino State Bank went broke, had plenty of money on deposit. But banks make money by borrowing money from depositors and lending it at a higher rate of interest to borrowers. In order the pay the depositors back the borrowers have to pay the money they owe the bank.

The Tenino bank's creditors could not pay their loans. The bank was unable to repay its depositors. Fearing a run on the bank, on December 6, 1931 the bank's Board of Directors voluntarily closed its doors and asked the state Superintendent of Banks to take over as receiver.

This marked the end of Tenino's period of prosperity. It was the event that gave rise to an innovative effort at financial self-help that helped pay off the bulk of the insolvent bank's debts and gave faltering Tenino worldwide fame.

The Citizens Bank of Tenino was not the only bank to crash. Other banks in the county also closed their doors.

Tenino citizens found themselves with goods to sell, necessities to buy and no money with which to trade. There was no deposit insurance prior to the New Deal of the 1930s. If your money was in the bank and the bank did not open, you had no money to spend.

Enter Don Major, the genius editor and publisher of the weekly Thurston County Independent, Tenino's newspaper.

Major had a printing press and an idea. He knew from talking with the state-appointed receiver that depositors were certain to get at least 25 per cent of their deposit accounts – eventually. Major convinced the Tenino Chamber of Commerce to issue its own paper money. This was scrip, in denominations of 25 cents, 50 cents and $1. The Chamber of Commerce guaranteed payment. The promise was backed up by an assignment to the Chamber of 25 per cent of the unpaid deposits of participating citizens.

It worked this way: If you had $400 on deposit with the failed Tenino bank, you gave the Chamber of Commerce a collateral assignment of the first $100 to be paid to you when the bank liquidated its assets. In return you got $100 worth of Tenino Chamber of Commerce scrip. Local merchants, desperate for business and willing to trust in the eventual redemption of the scrip, accepted it just the same as cash.

All of $1,279 in paper scrip was printed and issued.

It was accepted by local merchants. But paper money is easily counterfeited, and it wasn't as durable as the paper money printed by the government.

In 1997 Art Dwelley, then-editor of the Tenino Independent, told how the wooden money enterprise got started. In 1931 after the bank crashed Don Major decided to print his own Christmas cards on slicewood, a thin single veneer piece of wood then manufactured in the Grays Harbor area and used in making up the fragile wooden boxes that you bought your strawberries in at the grocery store. As a gag, Major put the plates for the Chamber of Commerce paper money on the press and printed one 25-cent certificate on a piece of the slicewood. Then he walked across the street to the Jiffy Lunch and presented it in payment for a nickel cup of coffee. The coffee shop crowd thought it was an interesting gimmick and before long the Chamber Board of Directors authorized printing a few more. Tenino's wooden money proved popular.

But the single-veneer wood proved fragile. It fractured easily along the grain. Someone decided to laminate the wooden currency by using two sheets of cedar or hemlock with a sheet of bond paper glued in between them.

By February 1932, the Chamber of Commerce directors decided to get into the money business big-time. Cash-starved local merchants accepted the wooden shinplasters readily.

A news story in the Tacoma News-Tribune made the Associated Press wire. The Universal News newsreel folks sent a camera crew to Tenino twice. Demand for Tenino's unique wooden money came from around the world. Contemporary accounts indicate would-be collectors included King Farouk of Egypt and Benito Mussolini, dictator of Italy.

Would-be brokers offered to buy all the wooden money the Chamber of Commerce could print at a discount of 25 per cent. The Chamber stuck by its guns and decided to sell the wooden money at face value.

The Chamber of Commerce printed and circulated eight separate issues of wooden money, most of it in 25-cent denomination, between February 1932 and January 1933. Of the initial issues, the three Chamber of Commerce trustees, Major, Dr. F. W. Wichman, Tenino's physician, and Dr. Al W. Meyer, Tenino dentist, personally signed each wooden certificate. The signing became such a chore that later issues of Tenino's wooden money had the signatures printed instead of hand-signed.[1]

Tenino is credited with the being the first to issue wooden money. Blaine, Wash., followed in 1933. Its money showed the Blaine Peace Arch. Olympia's Chamber of Commerce printed wooden 25-cent pieces in the shape of an oyster shell. This was called "oyster money."

Of the early paper scrip, $1,279 was circulated and $1,079.75 was redeemed. Of the wooden money, a total of $10,308 was issued. But the money was prized primarily as a collector's item. Only about $40 was ever redeemed.

---

[1] Money was not the only thing Tenino printed on wood. In 1933 the Tenino Telephone Company printed its telephone directory on one side of 8 x 12-inch sheet of laminated slicewood.

What did the Chamber of Commerce do with the rest of the proceeds? It used some of the profit to buy the old Citizens Bank of Tenino building from the bank's receiver. That helped push to redemption paid to depositors up to somewhat more than 70 per cent of the amount of their deposits. The building later was sold to the town for $2,400. It housed Tenino's town offices, a real estate office, an insurance agency, and a dental office and for some years was home to the Tenino-Oakville Bank. Other proceeds were used to help the unemployed and for a business loan in an attempt to restart the local stone quarry industry.

In 1935 the Chamber of Commerce also printed wooden 1/5-cent state tax tokens, after the state of Washington required collection of the tax but couldn't provide enough tax tokens to do the job. Later local leaders formed the Tenino Wooden Money Society and in the 1970s, 80s and 90s sold commemorative issues.

Today, original Tenino wooden money is worth much more than its face value. One Internet wooden money site says rare Tenino pieces can be worth up to $400. In 2005 one Internet seller offered a $1 Tenino wooden money piece for sale at a price of $150.

Don Major's original snapper press, on which the money was printed, and a fine collection of Tenino's wooden money, is a part of the exhibit at the South Thurston County Historical Society Museum at Tenino.

2

THE QUARRIES

The premier industry of Tenino from the 1890s through the start of World War I was its stone quarries. In the years before the War, the Morning Olympian frequently referred to Tenino as "the Sandstone Metropolis" and "Stone City." There were seven, and possibly eight, stone quarries in the Tenino area. The seven quarries we are sure of and the dates of their founding are:

Manville Quarry, a sandstone quarry located one-half mile north of Plum Station on McCorkle Road, sometime prior to 1888.

The Tenino Stone Co. quarry south of the old Northern Pacific main Rainier line tracks at the south edge of Tenino, in the fall of 1888.

The Eureka Sandstone Company quarry, later Hercules Sandstone Co. Quarry No. 2, northeast of Tenino in the Cattail District, 1889.

Hercules Sandstone Co. Quarry No. 1, on Lemon Hill west of Tenino, 1903.

Hercules Sandstone Co. Quarry No. 6, a granite quarry located about 3 miles east of the later-constructed Skookumchuck River Dam, 1915.

An unnamed deposit of granite just to the east of Hercules Quarry No. 6 on the Skookumchuck River, opened in 1936 and used for stone to complete the Grays Harbor jetty project that was stopped in 1916.

An unnamed granite quarry of limited production near the Olympia-Tenino Highway just north and west of the Burlington Northern Pacific Railroad overpass north of Tenino. This stone deposit was discovered in 1935. It was opened in the final months of World War II by the Army, which set up a short-lived school to train Army construction crews in extraction and crushing of rock and road building. The Army started the construction of barracks and accessory buildings in June 1945. Part of the training was carried out at the Hercules Quarry No. 1.

The Manville sandstone quarry operated only briefly. The quarry site later was covered by the realignment of what now is McCorkle Road. Its location was authenticated by David A. Knoblach, Washington state stone industry historian, who found a piece of sandstone pierced by a drill hole at the suspected location.

The first quarry in Tenino was the Tenino Stone Co. quarry. This quarry was developed by S. W. (Wes) Fenton and George N. Van Tine, quarrymen from Minnesota who had come to the area to look for possible sources of building stone. While in the area they found that local farmers had built fireplaces from chunks of sandstone they hacked with hand axes from sandstone boulders near Tenino. Van Tine and Fenton selected the deposits at the south edge of Tenino for development in part because they were close to the Northern Pacific Railroad tracks. They leased the land, which then belonged to Charles Billings, and opened a quarry in 1888 that they initially worked with a horse-powered derrick. This quarry was a cut stone quarry. It was varyingly known as the Van

Tine Stone Co., Van Tine & Fenton Stone Co., the Russell Quarry, the Tenino Stone Quarry Co., Tenino Stone Quarries, Inc., and the Tenino Stone Co. It will be referred to in this book as the Tenino Stone Co.

In 1950 the deep water-filled hole left after extraction of stone ended became the town swimming pool. Its old office building now is known as Quarry House and is used for community gatherings.

The second quarry, developed by the Eureka Sandstone Co., was a cut stone quarry north and east of town. It opened in 1889 and produced dimension stone for the Pierce County courthouse and the Northern Pacific Railroad warehouses in Tacoma as well as other structures before closing in the late 1890s.

David A. Knoblach, the geologist and historian, says there were three principal reasons why people of that period built of stone: (1) Stone and brick imparted an aura of permanence and prosperity, and stone was superior to the brick of the period; (2) In the Eastern states, lumber was scarce and stone and brick was not; (3) Wooden buildings burned readily and stone buildings did not. After much of Seattle burned in 1889 there was an almost frantic desire in Washington state for stone building material.

Sandstone also was used for street paving blocks, until replaced by granite paving stones and later macadam (asphalt) and concrete.

My grandfather, William McArthur, Hans P. Scheel and their principal partner, Claus Clodius, were big players in the local stone quarry business. William McArthur had worked in a stone quarry near Bannockburn, Scotland, before he emigrated to the United States in 1887. He came to Tenino some time in 1888 and worked as a foreman in the Tenino Sandstone Co. quarry. His brother, Andrew McArthur, another quarryman, came to Tenino from Scotland in 1889. A third brother, Robert McArthur, came some time before 1896.

It took a while for the Depression of 1893 to reach the West Coast, but when it did, the quarry where William McArthur was working closed down and he wound up in Salmo, British Columbia, Canada. During at least part of that time, he was working in a silver mine at Ymir, nearby. The family returned to Tenino in 1903.

Upon his return to Tenino, William McArthur, H. P. Scheel and Claus H. Clodius went into business together. Initially the company was called the Tenino Sand Stone and Townsite Company. It changed its name to the Tenino Sandstone and Townsite Company and then the Tenino Sandstone Company. Early advertisements showed Scheel and the company office at Spokane. W. L. Cadle, first of Seattle and then of Chicago and F. Swonson, Spokane, were listed as vice presidents. In early years the company's letterhead showed Cadle as general manager and William McArthur as superintendent. Cadle and Swonson were early investors who later left the company. The Tenino Sandstone Company was confusingly similar in name to the Tenino Stone Company. In 1907 the business changed its name to the Hercules Sandstone Co.

At its creation the company was aptly named. In addition to the stone deposits on Lemon Hill, the new company bought all of the platted and unsold land in the western part of what now is Tenino from the developers of the Snyder and Stevens Addition to Tenino.

Although Quarry No. 1 was not opened until 1903, the stone deposits were known and their exploitation planned many years earlier. The plat of the Snyder and Stevens Addition shows, in addition to the lots and blocks extending west from Ritter Street across Scatter Creek, more than 30 acres marked on the original map as "stone quarry."

Scheel, a native of Germany, came from a stonecutter family. (A fuller account of the career of H. P. Scheel in the stone industry is contained in Chapter 24.) He had worked in one of the Tenino quarries in the 1890s with William McArthur and later owned an interest in a large building and monument stone quarrier and fabricator in the Spokane area. That likely became their connection with Clodius, who was a banker in Ritzville, Washington. Clodius did come to Tenino occasionally. But he took no active role in the operations of the business.

Scheel was the salesman and entrepreneurial spirit for the company. William McArthur ran the quarry operations. The Scheel family owned property north of town, but lived in a large home in Tacoma's north end. Scheel had a room and took meals at the McArthur home when he was in town during the week. Clodius provided the bankroll that got the business started.

In 1903 Hercules Sandstone Co. opened a new cut stone quarry on Lemon Hill west of Tenino. It soon became a primary producer of cut sandstone on the West Coast.

McArthur family tradition had it that William McArthur ran the company. He did not. In the 1950s my uncle, Avard Mandery, found a ledger book for the Hercules Sandstone Company in the rear of the garage at the McArthur house on Sussex Avenue. It showed that each month when distributions were made to the shareholder/officers, Clodius got one-half, Scheel got one-third and William McArthur got one-sixth. During most of the years of its existence the company's letterhead listed Clodius as president, Scheel as secretary-treasurer and William McArthur as vice president.

Cut dimension sandstone was widely used in commercial buildings of the day. The Hercules Sandstone Co. produced stone for a number of commercial and government buildings in the western United States.

Tenino sandstone became the hallmark of quality in American building stone. The two Tenino quarries were intense business rivals. The older Tenino Stone Co. marketed its stone as "The Original Tenino Stone."

The stone was cut from the huge rock deposit by a channeller, a huge machine with rotating arms that dug a narrow ditch 52-inches deep around the side and ends of the block of stone to be quarried. Workmen used long-handled spoons to keep the channeller cut clear of dust and rock chips so the channeller could get a good cut on its next pass. Then the quarry workers would drill horizontal holes about 10 inches apart under the bottom and using sledge hammers and expanding feathers and wedges or light charges of explosives they would break it free. That was called a "lift".

The quarrymen originally drilled holes by hand. One man would hold the drill and a second would strike it with a sledgehammer. The drill was rotated a quarter turn between blows. The channeller first was powered by steam. Later both drills and channellers were powered by compressed air.

The stone was then hoisted onto cars and wheeled to the cutting shed where it was sliced and planed into the desired size. The cutting was done with a gang saw. But these saws didn't have teeth. They had a smooth cutting edge. The stone actually was cut by steel and lead shot (the quarrymen called it "chat") spread between the saw edge and the stone. The shot was in a watery slurry that was pumped into an overhead hopper by a chat-pump. Then it drained onto a latticework grid that distributed it over the width of the block.

The heavy blocks of stone were lifted by derricks. When a new boom was needed for one of the derricks, William McArthur would call on the nearby Jonis spar mill. Isadore Jonis would go into the woods, select a good tree, have it felled, peeled and trimmed so it had eight sides. Then the quarry crew would mount it.

At the top were the pulley blocks through which the cables ran. The blacksmith made steps—like over-sized staples—that were driven into the top side of the boom. Twice a day an oiler would climb to the top of the boom, and lubricate the pulleys. (Larry Scheel said they called it "oiling the rooster.") There was no safety gear. The oiler knew to hang on.

The 1906 earthquake in San Francisco destroyed most of the commercial buildings in that city. One of the few major buildings to escape the quake and the fire that followed was the Calvary Presbyterian Church, which had been built from Tenino sandstone. There is no indication that the stone of which it was built saved the church from quake and fire. But the miracle of survival was enough for those who had lost their buildings and didn't want it to happen again. Tenino sandstone became San Francisco's building material of choice. This brought a flood of orders as San Francisco set about rebuilding its city.

Architects' drawings specified the number and dimension of the various stones used to construct the exterior walls of the new buildings. Each stone was cut to size, marked and sent to San Francisco by rail. There, a crew of three Hercules Sandstone Co. men worked to match the stones upon their arrival with the architects' plans. Two of H. P. Scheel's sons, Karl and Walter, worked as apprentices in San Francisco for the company for several years.

Originally the identifying number of each individual stone was carved into the stone by hand. Later, the number was painted on. In earlier days when workmen were paid by the piece, the carver or cutter would cut his initials in each stone. Crews doing restoration work on the state capitol building at Olympia after the February 28, 2001 earthquake uncovered painted identifying marks.

The highest paid men in the quarry were the stonecutters. Many of them were immigrants from Scotland. These men belonged to the Journeymen Stonecutters Union of North America. They worked an eight-hour day and got better pay than the other men. The rest of the employees worked 10 hours. The stonecutters also traditionally wore a shirt and a tie while on the job. The other workmen did not. Dad said William McArthur and H. P. Scheel used to complain about the union men and how much they had to be paid. The stonecutters laboriously carved the ornate decorative stones used on the buildings' exteriors. They used wooden mallets, steel hammers, chisels and rasps and compressed air tools. Sometimes the work would be near completion when a mistake was made or a piece would break off. The stone was then broken and dumped behind the cutting shed and the work started all over again. They called these ruined stones "sparls". All blocks of decorative and dressed stone were packed for shipment in individual boxes lined with excelsior.

Larry Scheel, H. P.'s son and one of the last of the old-time stonecutters, said that some cutters, during idle time on the job, would knit to keep their fingers supple. The tools used in the quarry were of tempered steel. The blacksmith was an important man. He made many of the tools and kept the tools sharp and tempered. He had one or two helpers. The blacksmith would heat the metal red-hot in the forge, lay it on the anvil and then with a light hammer tap where it was to be struck. Then the helper, who did the heavy work, would strike it with a heavy hammer.

The two-story Hercules Sandstone Co. office was built of cut sandstone on the flats below Quarry No. 1 in 1913. It later was taken apart and reassembled on the town's main street to become the city hall, jail and library. The concrete slab where the building originally sat can still be seen below the quarry.

The bottom floor was the drafting room. It had a row of drafting tables with architects' drawings tacked to them. The company offices were on the second floor. The upstairs walls were paneled with two-inch thick slabs of dressed sandstone.

Tenino sandstone was particularly suited to construction work. Tenino stone is soft in composition. That makes it easy to cut and to shape. It hardens after its exposure to air. Its durability is proven by century old buildings still intact. William McArthur devised chemical treatments with waterglass (sodium silicate) that sealed the surface of the newly cut stone making it more impervious to moisture. A treatment of diluted phosphoric acid (one part of acid to five parts of water applied for five minutes) prevented it from changing color as it aged.

Stone from the Tenino quarries was grand stuff, indeed. At the Alaska-Yukon-Pacific exposition in Seattle in 1909, the Hercules Sandstone Co. showed a cut stone slab of Tenino sandstone that was 4 feet 6 inches wide, 8 feet 4 inches tall and only one inch thick. The slab was suspended in the air. By the end of the exposition, it had bowed eight inches due to gravity. But it showed no cracks. A picture of this slab appeared on the reverse side of the company's letterhead for years afterward.

At the exposition the Hercules Sandstone Co. was awarded a silver cup for its "flexible sandstone". Hercules was not the only local producer to be honored. The competitor Tenino Sandstone Co. won a silver medal for its Tenino sandstone at the Universal Exposition in St. Louis in 1904.

About 1910 the market for cut dimension sandstone began to fail. New construction designs called for taller buildings with a support of steel girders. Volume production of concrete began in 1906. Rotary mixers could make concrete of uniform composition on site, and it was cheaper than cut stone shipped from a distance.

Some buildings of this period were made of concrete blocks – called "cast stone."

The Hercules Sandstone Co. looked for new markets.

About this time, the Army Corps of Engineers announced it was going to rebuild one of the jetties that kept open the shipping channels at the mouth of Grays Harbor. Specifications called for the use of large boulders of sandstone. The Hercules Sandstone Co. bought the defunct Eureka quarry northeast of Tenino and entered a successful bid to produce 375,000 tons of rubble stone to be delivered in 1911 and 1912 for the repair of the jetty.

This was the first rubble stone contract entered into by the Hercules Sandstone Co. and marked the beginning of the end for the company.

There are two kinds of quarried stone -- cut (or dimension) stone and rubble stone. Previously, the Hercules Sandstone Co. laboriously cut stone blocks from the huge mass of virgin sandstone. The stone produced for the Grays Harbor jetty contract was to be huge, rough boulders. Now, explosives took the place of fine tools.

Ever appreciative of what the popular press might do for business, the Hercules Sandstone Co. dug 1,400 linear feet of 3-foot tunnels—called "coyote holes—through the face of what originally was a cut stone quarry. A crew of experts from the Dupont Powder Co. of Dupont, Washington, spent a week packing the tunnels with 43,100 pounds of black powder and 1,200 pounds of 60 per cent dynamite and stringing the electric wires that would be used to set it off.

On February 17, 1912 a special train brought spectators and officials of the Army Corps of Engineers from Seattle. A movie camera crew from the Motion Picture Advertograph Co. of Tacoma arrived to film the event. Folks in Tenino were warned to take all their fragile possessions down off the shelf. At 2:25 o'clock that afternoon, Major J. B. Cavanaugh of the Army Corps of Engineers, the man who approved the government contract, pressed the electric button. The charge was fired.

The resulting explosion was trumpeted as the largest single explosion in Washington State history.

It well may have been. The town shook. Huge clouds of smoke and dust arose. Newspapers reported that the explosion loosened 800,000 tons of rock. The Morning Olympian declared that "its most unique feature was the almost absolute absence of any noise or concussion. The load was so arranged by expert engineers that the noise and danger was minimized, scientific care being exercised by everyone employed."

The newspaper was a bit rosy in its reporting. In fact, the quarry's railroad spur was buried under rock. Holes up to 10 feet in diameter were punched in the buildings at No. 2 quarry.

Afterwards, the official party adjourned to the Oasis Hotel where 102 persons enjoyed a celebratory dinner at which 25 men—only one from Tenino—were listed as giving speeches. The dinner menu was a monument to boosterism. It featured: Olympia Oysters (Cocktailed with Tenino Booster Spirit), Consommé A La Sandstone, Chicken (with Hercules Sandstone Noodles), Cold Roast (with Sea Board Oil), Browned Potatoes (with crushed Steel), Celery and Lettuce (Grown on Mount Mullaney), Lemon Pie (Keithahn Cream with DuPont Powder Cakes), Tea, Coffee, Wine and Homespun Cigars (Of Hercules Strength).

The district engineer of the Corps of Engineers was impressed, as were the gathered reporters. Townsfolk who got dusted by flying rock dust, though not injured, were likewise impressed.

But 40 per cent of the rock blasted loose was shattered by the force of the blast into pieces too small for use. The company had the expense of pushing some and hauling the rest out of the way to make room for the useable large boulders loosened by the explosion.

The shattering of blasted rock should have been a warning. A repeat of this experience in the granite quarry -- No. 6 up the Skookumchuck River — some four years later would portend the end of the company and the financial destruction of William McArthur and H. P. Scheel.

The huge sandstone boulders were placed on flat cars and hauled to Grays Harbor where they were loaded on barges and carried to the final place of deposit on the rebuilt jetty. Despite problems at the quarry and a delay caused by the loss of the Corps of Engineers pile driver at the jetty, the Hercules Sandstone Co. delivered over 387,000 tons of stone during the 1911, 1912 and 1913 construction seasons.

While both Quarry No. 1 and Quarry No. 2 were in full operation, as many as 160 men were on the company payroll locally. The Hercules Sandstone Co. expanded its holdings. The company bought an existing dimension stone sandstone quarry at Wilkeson, Washington and named it Quarry No. 3. It opened a granite stone quarry at Ymir, British Columbia which became Quarry No. 5.

The company also claimed a Quarry No. 4. Dad said Quarry No. 4 was a granite quarry at Index, east of Everett. David A. Knoblach says he believes Quarry No. 4 was at Index. But the local historical society in the Index area says it knows of no ownership interest of either the Hercules Sandstone Co., Scheel or McArthur in the granite quarry that operated there from 1903 to about 1930. The company's business letterheads in both 1912 and 1914 indicated no quarries at Index, but it did list Quarry No. 4 at Tenino. If there was another Hercules Sandstone Co. quarry operation in the Tenino area, it remains unsubstantiated.

Quarry No. 4 may have been planned but never opened on a hillside located about a mile north and west of the west end of McIntosh Lake. William McArthur bought 40 acres of property there in 1912. Opening a stone quarry was an expensive undertaking. The heavy-duty truck was unknown in those days. It required construction of a railroad to the site before any product could be removed from a quarry.

Then, in 1915, The Hercules Sandstone Co. made its big, and fatal, move. H. P. Scheel's son, Walter, then 23 years of age, went hunting up the Skookumchuck River south of Tenino. He came upon a huge ledge of granite stone, at the foot of which was a jumble of huge rocks. The Army Corps of Engineers was now demanding stone that was more durable than sandstone. Granite fit the bill. The Hercules Sandstone Co., and some of the experts that it brought in to view the site, figured that the entire first year's contract requirement could be made up from the boulders that lay at the foot of the cliff, without the necessity of blasting.

Just getting to the site of proposed new quarry was a challenge. The rough trail from the end of the county road crossed the river several times. Walter Scheel, a bear of a man, picked up the experts and government engineers who went on an inspection tour and carried them one by one piggyback across the river.

Although it was not a part of the contract, the Army's Division Engineer, Lt. Col. J. B. Cavanaugh, apparently indicated that the Corps of Engineers had long been looking for a deposit of stone of the quality found at Quarry No. 6. He said that many years' of work was needed to restore the two Grays Harbor jetties. The chance to tie into many years of profitable production from Quarry No. 6 caused the Hercules Sandstone Co. to extend itself dangerously to get into production.

Contract in hand, the company set about opening the deposit.

This required building a 12-mile railroad spur from the Northern Pacific line between Tenino and Bucoda to the quarry site, which was accomplished in six weeks at a cost of $200,000. Part of the route was laid over the old Blumauer Lumber Co. logging railroad. About two miles of the Blumauer road was straightened and another six miles of new railroad was built. The company was in a hurry. It paid a premium price for right of way across farmers' land to gain access to the stone deposit. A mineral lease was signed with the Weyerhauser Company, owner of the land. Derricks and other equipment were hauled in from the idle Hercules Quarry No. 2.

Hercules Quarry No. 6 was intended as a rubble stone quarry. But its owners were looking to the cut stone market as well. There were at least two pieces of cut stone made from Quarry No. 6 granite. One was the Washington State marker made a part of the Washington Monument in Washington, D. C. Visitors to the Washington Monument can see it today. It is on the interior of the monument, about one quarter of the way down the monument's 898 steps. The other was a miniature grave marker, marked "Grand Canyon Granite, Tenino, Wash." which now sits on the library shelf of my living room.

The company shipped its first rock from Hercules Quarry No. 6 on June 28, 1915.

Once a day the company would bring a string of empty railroad cars into the quarry and park them on a spur above the quarry. As they were needed, individual cars were rolled down to where they were loaded with rock. The Hercules Sandstone Co. bought the switch engine that was used to ferry cars to and from the NP main line from the Oregon-Washington Railroad Co. At the quarry there were three big booms and several smaller derricks used to move the rock. The rocks were lifted with a pair of tongs. The quarry men would chip out holes on each side of the rock, the tongs were inserted and then the rock was hoisted by cable onto the cars. The huge stones were laid on the flat cars and propped in place with smaller stones. Smaller rocks were loaded into cars that had planking around the sides. Once a day the company would send the cars down to Centralia where they were weighed and then shipped off to Grays Harbor and eventual placement in the Grays Harbor north jetty.

My Dad, Robert McArthur, then 15 years old, was hired as a timekeeper at Quarry No. 6 during the frenetic summer of 1915. He lived there in a tent.

At one time there were as many as 300 men on the job. The timekeeper had a board with a row of hooks on it. Each hook had a brass tag, numbered sequentially from 1 on.

In the morning as work began, each man would come and take his numbered tag off the board and carry the tag with him to the job. In mid-morning the timekeeper would go to the quarry and pick up the tags from each man there. In his time book he would make a vertical mark alongside each man's name. The tags were placed back on the board. After lunch the men would again take the tags with them. These were picked up in mid-afternoon by the timekeeper who made a horizontal mark in the time book. At the end of the week the timekeeper made out his report and sent it in to the office in Tenino where the checks were made out. If a man quit in mid-week, the timekeeper would figure out the man's unpaid time. He would carry it with him on the train to Tenino to get paid.

Laborers got 25 cents an hour and worked 10 hours a day, six days a week. They ate in the bunkhouse and washed themselves and their clothing in the river. The cook's name was Ryan. Dad ate with Ryan and his family because they ate better than the men.

Bad luck plagued Quarry No. 6. In December 1915 the river flooded, taking out one bridge and damaging a second. Believing no blasting would be necessary, the company had laid its railroad tracks near the base of the cliff. Blasting was required to harvest the stone, and the tracks had to be relocated. Then, as the Hercules Sandstone Co. had experienced at its earlier operation at Quarry No. 2, it found that the blasting left a large percentage of the stone shattered and too small to fit the government requirements. This rock had to be cleared from the area to allow work to continue.

On January 22, 1916 funds for the payment by the government were ordered frozen. All rivers and harbors projects were suspended because of the impending entry of the U. S. into World War I.

The Hercules Sandstone Co. limped along for another year before it collapsed.

The company looked for other revenue ventures.

Equipment for the manufacture of coal briquettes was installed at Quarry No. 1 in August 1917. The company proposed to extend its railroad line up the Skookumchuck valley to connect with the Majestic coal mine.

H. P. Scheel and William McArthur and a private investor from Seattle later that fall incorporated the Pacific Reduction and Chemical Corporation, a mining and smelting venture. Andrew McArthur and Wes Fenton reported to the Tenino News that Dad's uncle, another Robert McArthur, had found "a mountain of copper ore" in the Bald Hills.

Neither of these ventures panned out.

H. P. Scheel, who had personally guaranteed the company's notes, lost most of his assets. Among the losses was the family's mansion on Tacoma's Prospect Hill, which boasted room for family, four servants, a steam-heated greenhouse, and the first Cadillac motorcar on the hill. One of the few things left to the Scheels was the family farm north of Tenino, which was titled in the name of Scheel's wife, Frances.

It was the end of meaningful stone production from Tenino's quarries. Andrew Wilson, who had been the Hercules Company's prize stonecutter, bought Quarry No. 1 in 1922 and renamed it the Western Quarry. Production of stone from that quarry continued in fits and starts until about 1940, although the Western Quarry did produce a quantity of building stone in 1927 for buildings at Camp Murray.

George Van Tine in 1895 had sold his interest in the Tenino Sandstone Co., Tenino's original quarry, to Dr. Donald Russell and Thomas Russell. Russell and Fenton closed down full-time operations in 1913. That quarry operated whenever it could get an order until 1926, when it closed for good. One of the quarry's more unique sales was 3,000 sandstone holystones, then used to scour the wooden decks of U. S. Navy vessels.

Evidence of the demise of the cut stone industry was the decision of the Tenino School Board in 1924 to build its new high school out of brick because it was cheaper than Tenino sandstone. That building burned in 1962.

The Walker Cut Stone Co operated the last of the old-time sandstone quarries in Washington next to the Hercules Sandstone Co.'s old Quarry No. 3 at Wilkeson. The Walker quarry closed in the early 1970s. Shortly before it closed, it still featured a derrick powered by a steam engine.

William McArthur separated from his family and moved about 1922 to Seattle. He later worked in Mexico and returned to Seattle where he died in 1940. H. P. Scheel and his family returned to Tenino and remained on the family farm north of town. In late 1922 he and two of his sons dismantled the ornate two-story Hercules Sandstone Co. office located near Scatter Creek next to Quarry No. 1 and rebuilt it on Sussex Avenue in Tenino where it functioned for years as the town's city hall. Two steel cells were placed in the old drafting room on the first floor for use as a city jail. The town fire truck was parked to the rear. The offices upstairs were made over into the city clerk's office and library and the fine sandstone paneling covered over. Sheel's son Walter, who had helped build the building on its original site, said it was only time he ever built the same building twice.

David A. Knoblach obtained a copy of the Corps of Engineers correspondence file relating to the Hercules Sandstone Co. from the National Archives branch at Seattle. From 1924 through 1938 H. P. Scheel carried on a steady stream of correspondence with the Army Corps of Engineers and with Congressman Albert Johnson. He sought first to recoup from the federal government some of his losses, then later a government job and, finally, a federal pension. He was unsuccessful in all.

Work on the Grays Harbor jetty, which the Tenino quarrymen figured would become their fortune, was not renewed until 1936.

Ironically, the stone for the 1936 project was taken from the same ledge up the Skookumchuck Valley as Quarry No. 6. The site chosen for extraction was immediately to the east of Quarry No. 6. The stone was shipped to the main line by a two-mile extension of the Weyerhauser logging railroad to Vail which by then had been laid into the Mulqueen Valley east of the old quarry. Workers were hired under the federal government's Works Progress Administration program. They worked a 30-hour workweek to make the work last.

Scheel developed a modest sand and gravel business after the war but the family never recovered from the collapse of the Hercules Sandstone Company.

After World War II Quarry No. 1 sat idle until the 1950s when it was bought by Chester Wilcox, owner of the local lumber yard. Wilcox drilled a well, built a huge shed on the ledge where the last stone had been harvested, and tried growing mushrooms.

That didn't work and in 1992 he leased and later sold the quarry to the Louis Guinette Masonry Company. Guinette worked up the stone veneer of Tenino's new Puget Sound National Bank building from saw blocks left on the ground by Western Quarry Co. in the 1930s. Guinette had been working a stone quarry at Camas, Washington. He liked Tenino stone. His stonecutters liked it too. It split handily into fine veneer.

Douglas Remmick, owner of Northwest Stone Co. of Tualatin, Oregon, bought the quarry from Guinette about 1995. Remmick hired locals to split the stone and used a Ditch Witch mechanized ditch-digging machine to cut out quarry blocks. One of Remmick's projects was the repair of the Main Hall campus building at Central Washington University at Ellensburg.

The Marenakos Rock Center of Preston, Washington bought out Remmick and began limited production of stone from Quarry No. 1 again. What originally was a producer of stone for basic building purposes has become a boutique producer of cut and decorative sandstone for decorative architectural purposes and for the restoration of early buildings.

The caps to two of the Corinthian columns supporting the cupola of the Washington State Capitol were damaged in the earthquake of February 28, 2001. Replacements were cut by Keith Phillips, a custom stonecutter and husband of H. P. Scheel's granddaughter, who since 1991 has operated from Hercules Quarry No. 1. Sandstone in the original building came from the now-closed Walker Cut Stone Quarry at Wilkeson.

3
THE SAW MILLS

Tenino sits in what originally was a prairie, made that way by the indigenous Native Americans who burned it annually in their quest for food. The hills around the town were blanketed with huge trees. The coming of the railroad brought a means of turning the huge trees into money. Trees were harvested, cut into merchantable boards and beams and shipped to ready markets. By the turn of the century, there were several mills in the area.

The Beaver mill was at the south end of Tenino. Dad worked there after he got out of the Army at the end of World War I.

T. F. Mentzer, among his other ventures, had a mill in Tenino. The Mentzer mill and the Blumauer Lumber Co. both had their own logging railroads. There were no log trucks in those days. Trees were felled and limbed by hand and the logs dragged to the landing by ox teams or by cables attached to steam donkeys.

J. B. Jonis had a mill just west of the railroad tracks and north of the road that runs up Lemon Hill. Jonis' wife Mary was the granddaughter of Wiscom MacDoland, who came to the Puget Sound region in 1832 with a group of scouts to establish Fort Nisqually. The Jonis mill specialized in spars. For years the Jonis family was the leading producer in Washington State of timber sleds on which were mounted steam donkeys. When William McArthur needed a spar for one of the booms at a quarry, he would send a man with Jonis' son Isadore out into the woods. They would select the tree and Jonis would custom-fabricate a spar out of it.

The Jonis family owned two houses located just east of the railroad tracks on Sussex Avenue. The older folks were gone but Isadore and his brother Dousite (McGraw), both bachelors, still were in Tenino when I used to visit my cousins there in the 1940s. They still owned both houses. The two men, by then of advanced years, lived together in one of the houses. The other one was used to store their stuff.

The Jonis brothers did not have indoor plumbing and made do with an outhouse. It was behind the house they lived in, hidden from the street by a patch of blackberry bushes but facing west toward the railroad tracks. The door to the outhouse fell off and was not replaced. Isadore and McGraw could do their business in the outhouse and watch the trains roll by.

E. J. Bordeaux operated a mill west of town that employed 22 men. He opened a shingle mill east of Tenino in March 1914.

The biggest mill in the area was the Mutual Lumber Co. mill located at the south end of Bucoda. Mutual had extensive timber holdings in the hills above Bucoda. It had its own railroad. Mutual Lumber Co. operated its mill at Bucoda from 1902 through October 1912 when it, along with the old territorial penitentiary building, burned. The fire destroyed 3,000,000 board feet of lumber and left 150 men without jobs. Mutual bought the Mentzer mill and timber at Tenino and operated there until they ran out of timber west of Tenino in 1919. Then the mill was rebuilt at Bucoda. The Mutual mill closed for good in 1946. I visited there with my parents right about the start of World War II. I remember there were four steam locomotives deadlined in the old, grown-over rail yards north of the mill. The cabs had been filled with small wooden logs to keep vandals from stripping the controls. Each locomotive had a diamond-shaped smoke stack, just like in the cowboy movies. These engines were scrapped during the war.

Before World War I the Mutual Lumber Co. timber crews ran into patches of hemlock trees. There was no market for hemlock and the mill didn't want it. But the trees were in the way. So the hemlock was logged, the logs hauled on Mutual's logging train to Bucoda, run through the saw a few times to break them into manageable size and then fed into the wigwam burner. It was cheaper and easier to bring them to the mill and burn them there than to work around them in the woods.

There also was a big mill at McIntosh Lake north and east of Tenino. The lake became a great huge millpond. That mill had a work force primarily of Japanese workers.

After it was logged, some of the timberland was abandoned and allowed to go back to the county for unpaid property taxes. Some of it was divided into parcels by the timber companies and sold to folks who tried to farm it. It sold cheap. In both 1914 and 1923 the Weyerhauser Co. advertised cut-over timberland for sale at $5 per acre. Several men who worked at the quarries had small acreages on Blumaer Hill and other places that they were trying to convert from logged-over forestland to farmland. That's how the term "Stump Ranch" got its name. The first challenge to the would-be agriculturist was to burn, blast and dig out the huge stumps left behind by the loggers.

4

THE COAL MINES

Another natural resource that continues to contribute to the Tenino-area economy is coal.

Coal was found early in the Tenino area. At least one coal mine was located near Tenino as early as 1874. The first school, located on Frost Prairie south of Tenino in 1862, was called the Coal Bank School. (This school operated until 1941 when it was consolidated with the Tenino school district.) Coal Bank was the first name given the area and the voting precinct that encompassed what later was to become Tenino, as was the first post office situated south of what now is Tenino in 1860.

A coal mine was opened at Hurn, a half-mile from the townsite of Tono, in 1907. Coal was shipped by rail from Tono via the Northern Pacific and the Port Townsend Southern Railroad to Olympia where it was loaded on ships for San Francisco.

There were at least two operating coal mines in the immediate Tenino area before World War I. The Black Bear mine was located near the cemetery on what now is Northcraft Road. This mine was owned by the Tenino Coal and Iron Co., William McArthur and developers from the Tacoma area. The Great Western Mine, later known as the Keystone mine, was on the west side of Colvin's

Prairie behind the Colvin house. This mine was opened by the Great Western Coal, Development and Mining Company, which originally had its home office in Seattle. It was foreclosed on for debt and sold at a sheriff's sale in March 1908. It later was sold for $35,000 to William McArthur who organized a syndicate that operated the mine for a brief time until it closed.

Both were operating mines and sold coal to the railroads. Both mines had railroad spurs to them.

There was a third mine near the Sumption place in Section 17 northeast of Tenino, but Dad said he wasn't certain it ever got into operation.

The mines operated with difficulty and produced low-grade soft coal. Both had problems with flooding from the high underground water table, which the pumps had difficulty clearing from the mines. One of the two operating mines ultimately burned. The other one had inadequate shoring and "squeezed" shut.

One of the problems of coal production in the Tenino area was that mine operators attempted to mine low-value coal in the conventional manner by sinking shafts down to the coal layers and hauling the coal to the surface in carts. In the 1960s a huge open pit mine was opened near Tono, which is still operating today and fuels the huge Pacific Power generating plant.

William McArthur also had an interest in coal deposits near Tono.

5
OIL EXPLORATION

Speculators tried to find oil in and around Tenino on a number of occasions. At least one well was drilled on the John Sarver ranch west of Tenino as early as 1902.

There was other oil exploration activity both before and after World War I.

Several companies were formed around Tenino between 1914 and 1920 to drill for oil and gas. Investors in and outside the community bought stock. A stock exchange trading shares in a dozen oil companies operated at Olympia. For a while in 1915 and 1916 William Godsell sold securities in Tenino under the name of the Tenino Oil Exchange. The developers were all from out of town. They never found any meaningful amount of oil or gas, just investor money.

There were at least 10 oil development companies selling stock in the Southern Puget Sound area.

Companies drilling in the Tenino region included the Washington-Oregon Oil Co., Scatter Creek Oil Co., D. H. & J. Oil Co., Spokane-Tenino Oil Company, Paraffin Oil Co., Pacific States Oil Co. and the Crescent Oil Co.

The oil exploration mania spread from Tacoma to Centralia. Some suggested that Tenino be called "the Oil City."

William H. Mullaney, logger and Tenino's unofficial poet laureate, penned a song emphasizing Tenino's central role in the oil exploration. The tune is lost to history. But the words were memorialized in the April 15, 1915 issue of Maurice MacDonald's Tenino News:

TENINO'S THE NAME

Our neighboring towns have lately got the "oil bug" in their hats.
We must admit they have us skinned for sharps as well as flats;
But the oil is here in our precinct and hence we claim
'Tis the Tenino Oil Field!
TENINO, that's the name.

CHORUS

It's a long way to old Tenino,
Two score miles at least.
From our oil fields at Tenino,
By the compass, North by East.
But yet they claim our oil field,
Now, isn't that a shame?
'Tis just the Tenino Oil Field,
TENINO'S THE NAME.

A town from the county south of here also comes in for half,
"Centralia-Tenino Oil Field!"
Now wouldn't that make you laugh?
The "Tacoma-Tenino Oil Field"
And it are just the same.
'Tis the Tenino Oil Field!"
Tenino is the name.

CHORUS

'Tis the wrong way to Centralia
To lay a pipe line;
'Tis a cold day when Tacoma
Our oil will refine;
While ye hear our oil field nick-named
Does certainly look lame!
'Tis "the Tenino Oil Field"
TENINO'S THE NAME."

The Tenino News in November 1914 breathlessly reported oil of high quality was obtained at 1800 feet from the Crescent well on the Grand Mound prairie. But if oil was there, it was not in commercial quantities.

William McArthur, W. S. Fenton and H. P. Scheel formed the Paraffin Oil Company and drilled for oil both at Hercules Quarry No. 1 west of Tenino and at Quarry No. 2 northeast of Tenino.

The Paraffin Oil Co. was founded in 1914 after an 810-foor exploratory well at Hercules Quarry No. 2 north and east of Tenino showed traces of oil. The Morning Olympian quoted Scheel as having found evidence of oil after the Big Blast of February 17, 1912. Scheel told the Olympian he also had spotted oil seepages near Hercules Quarry No. 1 west of town.

McArthur, Scheel and Fenton were the only shareholders. Unlike other most of the other would-be oil developers, Paraffin was designed to find oil, not sell stock.

The big operator in the Tenino area was the Crescent Oil Co., which had over 10,000 acres under lease in the Tenino area. George A. Mottman, mayor of Olympia, was the president of Crescent Oil Co. But the mover and shaker of the company was Emery C. Williamson, an Olympia real estate broker, who was the secretary and principal spokesman of Crescent Oil.

Newspaper display advertisements boasted stud horse type

and the promise of a sure thing. Today, such claims would violate securities regulations. Then they were mere enthusiasm.

One boasted:

OIL NEWS

TODAY $1 MONDAY $5

NOVEMBER 1ST, OFF THE MARKET

Mottman quit the company November 23, 1914, and in a statement in the Morning Olympian said:

" . . . cheating oil companies by the wholesale, and selling stock to the unsuspecting public does not prove an oil field and will hurt and delay the legitimate development of the enterprise and hurt our fair city very much instead of benefiting it."

Breathless "almost there" articles appeared on the front pages of local newspapers following the day to day progress of Crescent's well four miles west of Tenino.

At mid-year Crescent Oil Co., averring that its well surely would produce volumes of natural gas, applied to the Olympia city council for a franchise to lay gas mains and provide illuminating gas to the entire city at half the rates then charged by the Olympia Gas Co., which made its gas from coal.

As tension grew over prospects of the Crescent well south of Tenino, the Paraffin Oil Company started redrilling an abandoned 800-foot hole it previously had sunk at Quarry No. 1 west of town. The Hercules Sandstone Company also owned a number of undeveloped lots in the Snyder & Stevens's subdivision in the west part of Tenino. It advertised in the Tenino News that it was withdrawing all unsold lots from sale. McArthur and Scheel felt certain that there was oil under the town. The ad boasted: "Watch for the gusher."

Other traces of oil reportedly were found by workers digging an irrigation ditch as a part of the Yelm irrigation project east of Lawrence Lake.

The wells did not gush. Drilling stopped. The ads ran no more. The would-be oil boom died.

The Tenino area was not the only place to show evidences of oil and gas. Similar finds were reported in the Mossyrock area of Lewis County and in the Hoh River country of Jefferson County. A like flurry of oil exploration activity occurred in the Willamette Valley area of Western Oregon about the same time.

Theories are offered to explain the failure to find the oil and gas then everyone felt was there. Maybe the gas came from non-commercial pockets of so-called "swamp gas." Maybe there are tiny pockets of oil – just like the fragmentary deposits of gold that pepper the country. Maybe the traces of oil that were found were nothing but drippings from the oil drilling rigs and other machinery.

Exploratory oil wells were drilled in the area in 1927 and again in 1957 without results.

No one has ever found any merchantable volume of oil or natural gas in the Tenino area, but the dream fired up a lot of enthusiasm.

6

THE QUEST FOR GOLD

Well, they found coal and looked for oil. Why not gold?

Would-be prospectors looked for gold in the Black Hills and Nisqually River basin in 1858 with no results.

But there are reports of at least two incidental finds of gold in the Tenino area, one as late as the 1920s.

Perry Crothers worked for the bank in Tenino before it crashed during the Depression. That was when the country was still on the gold standard. Banks would buy raw gold that was brought to them.

Perry Crothers said that in the late 1920s Dad's uncle, Bob McArthur, periodically came into the bank with free gold that he had found somewhere. The bank would weigh it, have it assayed and then pay him its value.

No one ever knew where Uncle Bob got the gold. He didn't tell anyone. But he didn't drive a car. So wherever it was it had to be within hiking distance of Tenino.

Some folks figured that maybe Uncle Bob found it on one of the creeks that fed into the Skookumchuck River. Bob McArthur had prospected the Skookumchuck basin and found copper deposits there. Others looked for gold in the Skookumchuck Basin. In

1906 the Skookumchuck Gold and Copper Co. was incorporated by an Olympia speculator.

However it may have been the same source that produced gold for Chinese railroad workers in earlier years. Art Dwelley in his history of Tenino said that in the late 1800s Chinese panned gold from what was called China Creek that comes from the north to feed into Scatter Creek just east of the Tenino-Olympia highway bridge at the north edge of Tenino. Chinese crews were used in construction of both the Northern Pacific Railroad and the Thurston County Railroad which ran between Tenino and Olympia. Contemporary accounts note Chinese railroad workers were camping "on the prairie" near Tenino in 1872.

Commercial gold deposits were developed in the Cascade Mountains in the early days of Washington Territory. Local histories of western Washington and Oregon report finds of gold in both the Cascades and the Coast Range.

7
TENINO'S TWO RAILROADS

The railroad is the reason for Tenino's being. The Northern Pacific Railroad was building a line north to Tacoma from the Columbia River. It shut down construction for the winter in 1872. A depot, a hotel, a store building and one or two houses were built at the end of the line. A town was started there. Come the spring of 1873 the tracks were extended north to Rainier and Yelm and its eventual terminus at Tacoma. The buildings stayed and became Tenino.

Folks in Olympia figured the seat of territorial government should have a railroad, so they set about building their own. This was the Thurston County Railroad. It was organized in 1872, but it was not built until late July 1878. Part of its final construction crew included 25 Chinese.

The Thurston County Railroad came to Tenino from Olympia. It originally was a built as a narrow gauge road. Narrow guage was cheaper. Its rails were spaced 3 feet apart instead of the standard 4 foot 8 inches. The name was changed to Olympia and Chehalis Valley Railroad Co. in 1881 and Port Townsend Southern Railroad Co. in 1891. (The owners toyed with the idea of extending the line from Olympia to Port Townsend, then the site of the U. S. Customs House and a seaport of some promise. They changed the name but never extended the tracks.) Passengers from Olympia would get off the Port Townsend Southern at Tenino and get on the Northern Pacific train. You can still see a part of the old right of way of the Port Townsend Southern west of the Tenino-Olympia highway near the Offut Lake turnoff.

The original Northern Pacific depot served both railroads. It was located on Park Avenue at its intersection with Olympia Street. Billy Huston's two-story hotel building and Fred Brown's store flanked it. Brown's was the first store in Tenino. The lumber from which it was built was milled in Tumwater and hauled to Tenino by wagon. That was the start of Tenino's business district. The Port Townsend Southern line came down what now is McDuff Road northwest of town, then ran over what later became the high school grounds to meet the NP line at about Howard and Park Streets. The PTS line crossed Sussex Avenue at about Ritter Street.

The Northern Pacific moved its depot south of town to Tenino Junction in 1890. There is some confusion as to the reason. Some say it was because the railroad tracks at the site of the old depot were laid on a grade and locomotives once stopped had trouble getting started again. Others say it was because the railroad had no room at the depot site for additional side tracks.

Whatever the cause, the depot moved and so did part of the business district. The local hotel primarily served travelers. It was moved on rollers to the Junction. Several other businesses followed. Both Tenino and Tenino Junction appeared as separate communities on maps of the early 1890s. After a while, the Tenino business district that remained behind began to move to Sussex Avenue. Most of the buildings that had gone to Tenino Junction were moved back to town.

The Port Townsend Southern rerouted its tracks to a terminus at the new station at Tenino Junction. Those tracks were laid on a partial fill and then a trestle on the present line of what now is the main railroad line west of Tenino.

In 1891 the Port Townsend Southern converted its track to standard gauge. That meant that freight cars could be switched between the PTS and NP tracks. Coal from the mine near Bucoda was shipped over NP and PTS tracks to load on ships at Olympia.

In 1912 the Northern Pacific started building its so-called "Water Line" from Tenino through Olympia Junction and around Point Defiance to Tacoma. NP took over the old PTS line. Part of the PTS right of way was kept. NP relocated the rest of it. The Grant Company of Tacoma was the contractor on the job. Its crews cut through the hill north and west of Tenino and hit a bunch of springs. This caused the hill to start sliding and was difficult to stop. The construction company filled up hopper cars and made the fill that's still a part of the roadway west of Tenino. It hauled more of the dirt and dumped it near Napavine. Still more of it went into a fill west of Offut Lake. Finally the crews dug or drilled and put in pipes to carry away the water that lay under the slide and that stopped the slippage.

The Point Defiance line was opened for business in December 1914. All of the main line traffic of the Northern Pacific, Great Northern and the Oregon-Washington Railroad and Navigation Co. was routed over the double track line. Passenger traffic over the original line through Rainier, Yelm and Roy was cut back to two trains a day.

But the main line still bypassed Olympia. Olympia business interests, desperate for a direct connection to the main line, raised $25,000 to help finance a spur line connecting the Olympia waterfront to the main railroad line at Olympia Junction. The Morning Olympian predicted that this new connection would make Olympia the principal shipping point for coal from the Tono-area coal fields.

With the new water-level line as its main line, Northern Pacific moved to a new depot building built in 1914 of Tenino sandstone on McClellan Street next to the new line. That depot was abandoned by the railroad when passenger service ended and was moved in 1975 to become what now is the South Thurston County Historical Society museum.

Northern Pacific for some years had a 45,000 gallon water tank on the Rainier line near the grade school. Water leaked out of it, and in the winter formed long icicles that sometimes would fall. Then the boys used them as play swords. When the station was moved to Tenino Junction the water tank was moved there, too. Northern Pacific had one man whose full time job was to keep the pump going to keep water in that tank. Steam engines didn't go far without loading up on water and a lot of the them stopped at Tenino.

There were 13 or 14 trains a day through Tenino. The steam engines sprayed cinders when they roared by. The boys would go down to the tracks to watch the trains go by. It was the most powerful thing in their lives.

When folks moved out of town, they moved their belongings by train. There were no moving companies in those days. A freight car would be shunted onto the siding and the family would haul its belongings down and load them on the car. They packed all the little stuff themselves in wooden boxes. Dad remembered that one family took its cow with them. They put the cow in the box car with their furniture. One of the boys rode with the cow and furniture.

8
TELEPHONES

T. J. McClellan built Tenino's first telephone system. That was in 1905. The town all watched while the crews strung the wires.

The first telephone exchange was in T. J. McClellan's drug store. At the start the switchboard could only accomodate five telephone calls at a time. There was one long distance line to Olympia and another to Centralia.

The William McArthur family had one of the phones. It was on a private line. That way no one could listen in on your business calls. The phones were old-fashioned magneto phones with a crank on the side. When you wanted to call someone, you lifted the receiver to see if anyone was on the line, replaced the receiver, and cranked twice. The operator would answer and you'd tell her who you wanted and she'd ring them for you.

In the early years, you never asked for the number. You just told her who you wanted to talk to. She knew the number. In 1924 the Tenino Telephone Co. printed a telephone directory and told its customers that thereafter they would have to ask for the number, not the name. The turn-the-crank telephone system remained in use until it was converted to dial in 1955.

The switchboard was open at night, too. The operator slept by the switchboard.

At one time there were three different companies providing long-distance telephone service. They were Pacific Telephone Co., Northwestern Telephone and Citizens Telephone. By 1913 the Tenino system was connected to Pacific Telephone and not to the others. The other companies served some towns that Pacific Telephone did not. In a landmark case affecting telephone service throughout Washington, Pacific Telephone was directed to allow the other long distance carriers to connect to the Tenino exchange.

Dad's cousin Bob McArthur—Andrew McArthur's son—worked for McClellan. He was in the process of buying the telephone system when he was killed in an automobile accident in 1923.

9

LET THERE BE LIGHT - ELECTRICITY CAME

T. J. McClellan also built Tenino's first electric light plant. This was in 1906, a year after he started the telephone company. Edith Newell, McClellan's daughter, wrote that the first power plant was next to the Blumauer mill at the south edge of town. Dad said he remembered the first light plant was in a building on property owned by William McArthur. The family later used it as a barn. The dynamo was mounted on a big concrete slab. This was near the railroad tracks and north of the new railroad depot. Dad did not remember whether the dynamo was powered by steam or a gasoline engine.

Later McClellan moved the plant to the north side of town. It was west of the railroad tracks to Olympia and just north of Scatter Creek next to Jonis' sawmill.

Initially, it was a poor system. The power went out frequently. Even when it worked, the lights likely were dim. The bulbs had carbon filaments in those days instead of tungsten, and didn't burn very bright.

There were overhead street lamps at most of the intersections. These were arc lights. The lamps had two pieces of carbon inside a glass bowl. Electricity arced between them when the power was turned on and that made the light. To service them the workmen would lower the lamps on a pulley and gap the carbon. When the carbon was burned out they would discard the pieces in the street and the kids would pick them up. The kids said you could write your name on the side of a building real well with one of those pieces of carbon.

The McArthurs didn't have electricity in the first house they lived in at 209 So. Wichman Street. But the big house they lived in at 158 So. Wichman Street had wiring on the first floor but not the second.

The first power poles had cross arms on them. Dad recalled they seemed a lot shorter than the poles are today. The electric system extended only to the city limits. Folks in the country still used kerosene lamps.

The power system later was sold to W. Dean Hayes and S. W. Fenton, then to North Pacific Power Co. and then Puget Sound Power & Light Co.

Most of the mills and quarries had their own electric generators. They were powered by steam. At the Hercules Quarry No. 1 the derricks and channelers at first were run by steam. In 1904 the company had a powerhouse built and equipped by the Olympia Light and Power Company. At first the dynamo provided only electricity for the lights and small equipment. In November 1911 the power company built a high-power AC transmission line from Centralia to Tenino. Then the company equipped the derricks with electric motor hoists and the channelers switched to compressed air that was made by an electric compressor. At the Skookum Mill south of town the generator powered only the electric lights. The saws and power equipment were all run by steam.

Dad recalled when the lights first were turned on in Tenino.

The McArthurs were living in the big house then. William McArthur had the house wired. Dad wasn't sure who did the wiring but thought it was one of T. J. McClellans' sons. McClellan had a large family. They turned the power into the lines and the lights came on. T. J. called William McArthur on the phone and said: "How are the lights over there, Billy?" McArthur, who tended to understate things, answered: "Well, I can see them."

The original power system was Direct Current. Today Alternating Current comes into the distribution system at a high voltage and then is stepped down by a transformer at each house. In the original system the generator put power into the lines at about 120 volts and it got weaker the farther from the generator it got. It was great if you lived in the west end of town. If you lived in the east part of town, away from the generating plant, your light bulbs glowed.

10

OUT OF THE MUD – PAVING THE STREETS

Originally, Tenino's streets were dirt. Mud in the winter and dust in the summer. Horses and wagons kept it churned up all the time.

In 1914 the town council paved the first street in Tenino. The main street was paved over a distance of a mile and a half from Lycan's corner, where the Tenino-Olympia highway and the highway to Rainier now join, to the south town limits on the road to Bucoda.

Downtown, from the intersection with Stage Street to the jog in the road by the bandstand at Ritter Street, it was paved curb to curb. The rest of the route was just an asphalt strip wide enough for two cars to pass. There was a debate about how wide to this strip ought to be paved. The council solved the problem by parking three cars next to each other and measuring them. That determined the width. This part of the road had concrete curbs that were set flush with the surface of the road. The asphalt was poured into the middle. This road followed the route of the present highway except that it jogged to the west on 5th Street and went south on what now is McClellan Street, then made a right angle turn west under the railroad underpass. Until it was resurfaced recently, you could still see the concrete curbs set flush in the ground on part of 5th Street.

The total cost of a project was about $35,000. The cost of the paving the intersections was met with proceeds from a $9,000 bond issue. The rest of the paving cost was paid by assessments against abutting property.

T. F. Mentzer and other property owners who were to be assessed for the cost sued to prevent the paving. They claimed that the assessment would equal the value of some of the property to be assessed. They lost.

Paving made sense. Town officials said it cost Tenino $2,200 the year before just to keep up the mud and gravel streets.

Just to make sure the contractor who won the paving contract did a good job the council hired one of the losing bidders to be Tenino's official inspector of the work.

At the time Tenino's principal thoroughfare was the main North-South road through western Washington. The state later paved the rest of it. Originally it was called the National Road, and where it came through Tenino it came up Park Avenue next to the old Tenino-Rainier railroad line. In the summer the National Guard company from Centralia would march through town to Camp Murray for summer camp. The Guard had horses and mule-drawn wagons for the supplies and equipment, but the men all marched. They used to stop by the Hercules Quarry No. 2 northeast of town to wash their feet in the creek.

When Sussex Avenue was paved, the town also put in concrete sidewalks. The rest of the original wooden sidewalks were taken up and replaced with sand and concrete walkways as part of a WPA project in 1935. Editor Don Major of the Thurston County Independent dourly commented:

"Men will be paid $44 a month for a thirty hour week—five

days of six hours.... In case of bad weather or not sufficient sidewalk work, pay will go on even if there is nothing to do."

Foreman of the crew was Andrew Wilson, the Hercules Company's former ace stone cutter, who apparently had plenty of time between intermittent orders at the former Quarry No. 1.

Rural roads were still mud. Sally Larson Bailey, H. P. Scheel's granddaughter, wrote that after World War I the Scheel daughters were ordered by their mother to wrap their shoes in burlap sacking to save them from the mud when they walked to school from their home north of town.

In part because too many people got hurt at the railroad crossings through Bucoda, the state about 1914 proposed to build a new highway from Centralia to Olympia. The highway engineers proposed to follow a route that is about the same as Interstate 5 today. Businessmen in Tenino didn't like that. Today, when the government wants to build a highway, people want the traffic to go through somebody else's town. Not then. Traffic meant people and people meant business. Tenino didn't want the highway moved. J. Dean Hayes, the president of the Tenino State Bank, was in the Legislature then. He fought the bypass of Tenino. The highway was rerouted to avoid Bucoda. But it continued to go through Tenino. The rerouted state highway was finished about 1922.

The worst part of the road between Olympia and Tenino was Chaen Hill. This section of the road has been realigned since then. It was a steep hill. Before the railroad came, teams hauling timber and farm goods to Olympia would double-team going up the grade. It was the scene of a number of accidents. Chaen Hill was quite a pull for the automobiles of the day. Some cars didn't have fuel pumps. Gas flowed by gravity from the gas tank, which generally was under the front seat, to the carburetor. If the car was heading up a really steep hill, gas wouldn't flow to the engine and the engine could stall. In that case, those people backed up the hill in reverse gear. Other cars had trouble making it with a full load. William McArthur would make the kids get out and walk up the hill while he drove. But going the other way he was afraid the mechanical brakes might fail so he would make the kids get of the car and walk to the bottom of the hill where he would pick them up again.

11

WHAT THEY DID FOR FUN

In those days people made their own entertainment. There was no TV and little else.

Dad's sister, Bernice (Bunny) Mandery, kept a diary covering her high school years from 1919 to 1922. She chronicled what she did each day. She wrote that spent a lot of time "visiting".

Dad, William McArthur and the other men of the family all belonged to the Masonic Lodge. Dad was the first man to be initiated into the lodge in its present sandstone Temple on Sussex Avenue. Margaret McArthur for years was the Chaplain of Tenino's chapter of the Order of the Eastern Star.

Tenino's Masonic Lodge was chartered in 1890 and its affiliated Eastern Star Chapter organized in 1893. The other preeminent fraternal organization, the Fraternal Order of Eagles, was formed in 1904.

The Boy Scouts were big. Tenino had the first troop in the area.

The biggest event of the year was the Fourth of July celebration. The whole town joined in.

A machinist at one of the quarries bored out a steel shaft and made a small muzzle-loading cannon out of it. The cannon was mounted on wheels. The cannon is now a part of the collection of the South Thurston County Historical Society Museum.

Each year on the night before the Fourth of July the cannon was hauled to the top of Lemon Hill and at the crack of dawn it was fired. That opened the festivities.

The highlight of the celebration was the annual parade. Business houses mounted floats, cobbled together on farm wagons and pulled by bunting-draped horses.

Up through about 1908 the parade marched west on Sussex Avenue. After that, since the whole town repaired afterward to the park, which was at the east end of town, the parade route was turned around and ran west to east.

The Tenino Cornet Band played.

Behind the band came a mock hospital tent set up on a flat wagon bed.

Behind that came Indian Louie Quityamals astride a white mule. Another mule pulled the homemade cannon. Behind the cannon marched the Tenino Drum Corps. There was at least one fifer, and two drummers. Wes Fenton played the bass drum.

Behind them marched the rag-tag members of the Tenino Home Guard. This group was intended to depict a local militia. Dad said short men carried long rifles, and tall men carried short rifles. Some were clad in remnants of cast-off military uniforms. One photo taken after the parade about 1906 showed one participant clad in the skirted coat and cocked hat of a naval officer of the Mexican-American War.

These were the principal participants in the Battle of Pea Soup, an annual event of epic proportion first carried out in 1893.

Periodically during the course of the parade, the hospital wagon, cannon and Drum Corps would stop. The cannon would fire (a blank, of course, accompanied by a lot of smoke). One of the members of the Home Guard would fall. His companions would hastily pick him up and deliver him to the hospital wagon.

Inside, the doctor—often Dr. F. W. Wichman, the town's physician—would saw through a board and toss a short length of 2 x 4 to which was nailed an old boot out the back of the wagon. This was to show that a field amputation had been performed.

The wounded man then sneaked out the front of the wagon and rejoined the Home Guard which marched another block and then did it all over again.

In addition to being the wounded hero, the member of the Home Guard who got carried to the hospital tent also got a shot of whisky out of the communal bottle maintained in the wagon.

William McArthur's brother (and Dad's uncle), Robert McArthur, was a member of the Home Guard. Uncle Bob liked to drink. One year he kept falling down when it wasn't his turn. The cannon fired. Uncle Bob fell down in the dirt of Sussex Avenue. He waited to be picked up and hauled to the hospital wagon for a shot from the bottle. And waited. When he looked up he found his companions had left him on the battlefield and the parade had moved off a block down the street.

After the parade the whole town gathered in the town park for a free clambake, band concert, ball game, visiting and dancing on the floor of the pavilion.

ENTERTAINMENT

Folks entertained a lot. The William McArthurs always had a full house at the holidays. There is a picture of the McArthur Christmas gathering about 1908 in the photo section of this book.

When the McArthurs entertained, a lot of their guests were Scotsmen. Uncle Jimmy Stevenson would play the fife and they would do the highland fling. Uncle Jimmy was an uncle of Andrew McArthur's wife, Jessie. He was a bachelor and a stone cutter.

William McArthur liked to dance the highland fling and the sailor's hornpipe. His brother, Andrew McArthur, would play the accordian. Dad said that after a drink or two they were quite good.

The party always wound up with a toast to the Queen. Dad said the toast was to Queen Victoria. But he wasn't sure why they always toasted her. She had died in 1901 before the family came back to Tenino from British Columbia. Dad said it likely was because Victoria was the ruling monarch when the families came over from Scotland. Or maybe it was because she was dead, and they were secret Scottish Nationalists.

BASEBALL

Baseball was the big sport for small towns in the years before World War I, and Tenino was no different. Tenino, Bucoda, Yelm, Rainier and most of the small towns in the area had their town teams. The teams would come to Tenino by train. The home town rooters came with them. The Tenino ball field was down where the high school was built in the 1920s. It had an 8-foot fence around it. Admission was 10 cents. Dad and his brother Bill were each given 25 cents to spend. The first 5 cents after admission was spent for a bag of unshelled peanuts.

BERRY PICKING

On the logged off land around the No. 2 Hercules quarry north and east of town there were lots of wild blackberries. These were the true wild blackberries – the little ones. Dad and his brother Bill would pick them and sell them to an old Indian woman in town. She would pay them 10 cents for a 5-gallon lard pail full of the berries. She would buy all that they could provide her. She made wine out of them. Sometime while the boys were out picking the weather would be hot and they would lie on their stomachs and drink out of Scatter Creek.

WHAT THE KIDS DID

Kids played together. Dad and his brother Bill were a year apart in age. They were inseparable.

Dad and Bill would go down to Scatter Creek and catch a mess of crawdads. They'd put them in a can of water, cook them over a fire and eat them on the creek bank.

In those days the salmon came up Scatter Creek to spawn. They would go as far as the Sumption farm at the foot of Chaen Hill. The salmon were pretty well beaten up by the time they got to Tenino. Often they were part way out of the water as they wiggled over the shallows. Sometimes the kids would pull them out of the creek and have a salmon roast by the creek north of town.

As kids, Dad and Bill sometimes would ride their bicycles to Centralia to buy a cream puff. The roadway was not fit for a bicycle. It wasn't paved yet. So they would ride their bikes on the railroad tracks. Cinders fell from the locomotives which made for a smooth path between the tracks. If a train was coming, they'd drag their bikes off the track and down the bank to let the train go by and then get back up on the track and keep pedaling until another train came along. There were 13 or 14 trains a day through Tenino in those days, so they had to keep a sharp lookout.

Dad said the cream puffs were worth the effort.

Other outings took Dad and Bill and their bicycles up Chaen Hill between Tenino and Olympia. They would push their bikes up the dirt road to the top of the hill, coast their bikes down the hill and then push them back up the hill again. There was a spring at the bottom of the hill. Sometimes they would make a cup out of skunk cabbage leaves and dip up water to drink. Other times they visited the Sumption farm where they could pull a bucket of water from the well and drink from the ladle.

One day when Dad was 12 and Bill was 13 Grandpa McArthur sent the boys to the mill to get some lumber. The boys took it to Jake Hartl, and he built the boys a rowboat out of the lumber. The kids had a burro named Cuddy. When the rowboat was finished, they put it on a wagon, hitched up Cuddy the burro and hauled it up to Offut Lake. They tied the boat up at Bronson's dock and left it there all summer.

The boys made many trips to Offut Lake on their bicycles that summer to spend the day with their rowboat.

Cuddy the burro was their favorite. Grandpa McArthur had the blacksmith make a three-wheel wagon. The boys hitched the burro to the wagon and drove it around the town. The burro, Dad said, was the joy of their lives.

The Northern Pacific built the stone depot on the new main line west of town. It had an indoor toilet. The railroad let the sewage drain down into the pasture where the family kept the burro. Cuddy drank some of the sewage and died.

Humor was good but crude. At Halloween Dad and his brother Bill tipped over outhouses, still in use at many Tenino homes. One year Bill slipped into a hole and ruined his new pair of shoes.

When they were in grade school, Dad and his friends used to go skinny-dipping in Scatter Creek. There was a swimming hole near the end of the Port Townsend Southern fill west of what now is Wichman Street. The hole was about chest deep and they could dive off the bank. The bigger kids would sometime grab the little kids and throw them in. Or they'd tie your clothes, which you had left on the bank, in knots and then wet the knots so you had a rough time getting your clothes untied. They called that "chaw beef." Once in a while the bigger kids would pee on the knots so you couldn't use your teeth to get them undone. It was a tough town and there were some tough kids in it. All 12 grades were taught in one school.

Some winters the weather was cold and things froze up. Kids experimented. They put their tongues on the railroad track on a freezing morning. The tongue sticks to the rail until the ice melts, and the tongue gets very sore.

Every once in while a traveling evangelist would come to Tenino to carry out his crusade in a tent. One evangelist had the ability to walk on the backs of the seats while he preached. Word got around and many of the kids played hooky from Sunday School to see a better show.

When Dad and his brother Bill were in high school William McArthur owned an interest in the Francis Hotel. On Saturday nights he'd let the kids go to the hotel and have a dance in the lobby. He'd have a cook there to fix something for the kids to eat. There really was little other entertainment in Tenino.

When the kids got older, every once in a while three or four of them would hire the town taxi to take them to Olympia for dinner and a movie. They would pay the taxi driver for the gas, take him to the show with them and buy his dinner.

Dad used to say that every time he heard the song "Meet Me Tonight in Dreamland" it reminded him of Peasley, the taxi driver. Except they called them jitneys in those days.

When Dad got older he and his friends would go in the evening to the prairie north of town, build a bonfire and have a wiener roast or a fish fry. There sometimes were 15 or 20 fellows there.

Sometimes someone would bring a sack of home brew. Dad said he never dared drink any of it. He was of age, but he was still living at home. Grandma McArthur was death on liquor and he'd have been in trouble had he come home with beer on his breath.

There were quite a few Italian immigrants in Tenino. Some did clean-up work at the quarries. Others worked in the mills. They all were bachelors and they lived in shacks south of town on the prairie. On Sundays they would bring their dirty clothes down to Scatter Creek, build a fire, surround it with rocks, fill a tub with water and set it over the fire and boil their clothes. They then would eat their lunch and take the clothes out and spread them on the grass to dry. Then they would stretch out on the grass and take a nap. That was their Sunday.

THE KU KLUX KLAN THAT WASN'T

One night about 1921, after the Ku Klux Klan started making a lot of news, some of the fellows went down to Scatter Creek and built a fire and walked around with bed sheets over their heads and with masks made out of sheeting with eye- and mouth-holes cut in them. The Catholics in town got nervous. Bob Shea was the manager of the garage where Dad worked. Shea was a Catholic. He was concerned about what was going to happen with the Ku Klux Klan. Dad didn't think any of the fellows were members of the Klan. They just did it for a lark.

DANCES

Dances were held at the rural dance halls every Saturday night. The band would play until late in the evening, and then break for an hour while most of the crowd went out into the parking lot to visit and drink. Then the crowd would take up a collection and if they collected enough money, the band would play until the early morning hours.

Edith McClellan Newell in her memoirs said that she, her brother Grover McClellan, Art Gilmore and Andrew McArthur's son Bob McArthur formed their own dance orchestra and sometimes played dances that lasted until 5 o'clock in the morning.

One night Dad had a "hot" date and borrowed a brand new Ford car from the garage to go to the dance at Fir Tree Lane. One of the locals who was quite a college football star had too much moonshine to drink. He threw up all over the fender of the car. The paint came off and they had to repaint the fender.

12
WHAT THEY ATE

In early day Tenino, butchers killed and cut up their own goods. When the butcher butchered a cow, the boys would go to the market and ask for the stomach, which they blew up and used as a football. The butcher would talk to the boys and kid with them while he did his work, and all of a sudden he would toss the stomach to them, splattering blood all over them. Then, Dad said, he would laugh. But the boys got their football.

There were no refrigerators at the time. Folks bought their canned and dried goods in advance and their fresh goods daily. Many folks had iceboxes. The blocks of ice were brought up from the ice plant at Centralia by train. Families would send the kids to the depot. They carried the ice home in gunny sacks. There was an ice plant in Tenino for a while, but when Prohibition came along it closed.

Folks seldom had fresh fish, because there was no refrigeration. Del Axtelle had the meat market in town. When he got a shipment of fresh fish in, he'd phone his favorite customers and tell them fish was in stock. Then they would tell him if they wanted any and he would deliver it to the house.

Metz Gill's dad used to go fishing for smelt. He'd bring them home, gut them and string them up on a line in the back yard.

When William and Margaret McArthur went to Tacoma to visit they always stopped at Roberts Brothers' grocery near Wright Park. Roberts Brothers specialized in imported merchandise. The folks would buy Scottish food that they couldn't get anywhere else. The old-timers enjoyed their Scots food. They said it reminded them of home.

The Scots weren't the only one with a taste for the foods of their homeland. H. P. Scheel's wife Frances trained under a chef in her native Germany. The Scheels ate a lot of traditional German fare.

Henry J. Keithan had a creamery on 6th Street at the south end of town. He opened the creamery in 1905. Every Saturday the farmers would come to town and sell him their cream. After World War I Keithan bought a truck and picked up the cream at the farm. Keithan made butter from the cream. He had a special wrapper under the trade name of Butter Cup Brand and he sold it in Tacoma. The creamery had a terrible smell. But the buttermilk was free. It was in a big vat and you could help yourself. You had to scoop the dead flies aside to dip it out. The hobos used to get off the trains and go to the creamery. Keithan would let them have all the free buttermilk they wanted.

Many families in town had their own cow. William and Margaret McArthur had a cow that was pastured on land that they owned west of the old house next to the railroad tracks. The kids would go to the pasture and bring the cow up to the house. Grandma McArthur would milk it and when she was finished the kids would take it back to the pasture and feed it.

PHOTOGRAPHS OF

EARLY-DAY

TENINO

White smoke curled upon from the exploding cannon as parade-goers fought the mock Battle of Pea Soup in the Fourth of July parade, 1906. Indian Louie Quityamals is astride the white mule at the left of the picture. The muslin-sided hospital tent is on the float ahead of the marching Tenino Home Guard. (Author's Collection)

Tenino produced its own clowns for the July 4 parade, about 1909. The clowns are unidentified. The burro is Cuddy, which belonged to Bill and Robert McArthur. (Author's Collection)

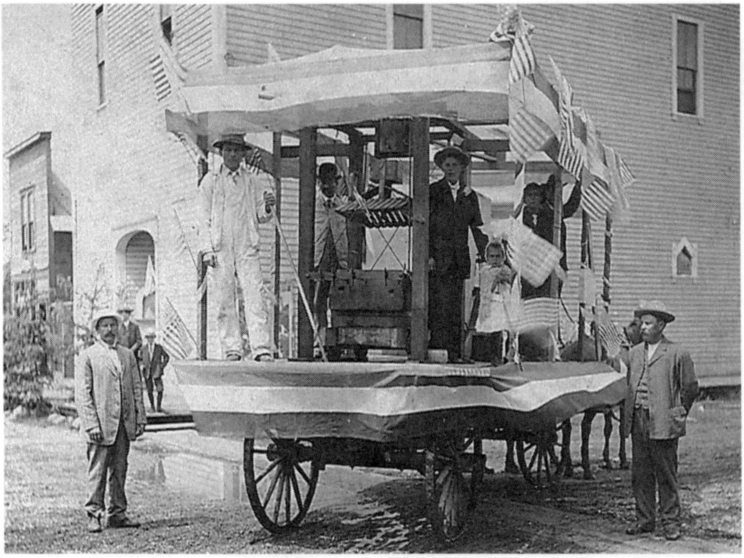

For the Fourth of July parade about 1905, the Hercules Sand Stone Co. built a miniature saw house replete with block of stone. Standing are Andrew McArthur (l) and William McArthur. On float (l-r) August Klingbiel, Phillip Lindau, Walter Scheel, Bernice McArthur and Roscoe Miller. (Author's Collection)

The Tenino Sandstone Co. mounted equipment, several employees and Indian Louie Quityamals on a float for the July 4 parade, about 1905. (Author's Collection)

At the Fourth of July picnic in the city park, 1907, Tenino posed for the photographer. Center are S. W. (Wes) Fenton (with the bass drum) and to his side Indian Louie Quityamals (with a star-spangled scarf about his neck). (Author's Collection.)

Beside the oven at the clam bake at Tenino's city park on July 4, about 1905. Standing (left with plate in hand) William McArthur. In uniform, Jake Hartl. (Author's Collection)

Hercules Sandstone Co. Quarry No. 1, Tenino, from the east, about 1904. In the foreground is the original railroad spur to the Port Townsend Southern Railroad. Later a spur line to the new PTS track, along which the present Burlington Northern runs, was built from the quarry to the south. (Author's Collection)

Hercules Sandstone Co. work crew on one of the first lifts shortly after the opening of Quarry No. 1 on Lemon Hill west of Tenino, about 1904. Note the old-fashioned steam channeller. Left-Right, top: Norm Clowers, John Maxwell, ____. Bottom: Bob McDonald, ____, William McArthur, ____. (Author's Collection.)

Work shed of Hercules Sandstone Co. Quarry No. 1, Tenino, where workmen shaped blocks of sandstone, 1909. Andrew Wilson, lead stonecutter, is in foreground. (University of Washington Special Collections, Neg. No. A. Curtis 14652).

Machine shop and crew, Hercules Sandstone Co. Quarry No. 1, Tenino, about 1909. (Author's Collection)

Stone cutting channeler at Hercules Sandstone Co. Quarry No. 1, about 1905. This was a steam-powered channeler. The steam came by hose from a stationery boiler. (Marenakos Rock Center Collection)

Steam-powered channeler at work a Hercules Sandstone Co, Quarry No. 1, Tenino, about 1907. This stone-cutting machine had steel digging tools attached to a flywheel on each side and dug narrow channels in stone bed, which later were broken free to form huge blocks of stone. The steam-powered channeler later was replaced by a machine powered by compressed air. (Joanie Guggenmos Collection)

This elaborately carved sandstone fireplace facing was the star of the Hercules Sandstone Co. exhibit at the Southwest Washington Fair at Centralia about 1911. You could have bought it for $45. (Author's Collection)

This photo, taken about 1911, was used to illustrate advertisements and the reverse side of the company letterhead of the Hercules Sandstone Co. The slab in the photo was 8-foot 4-inches by 4 feet in size and was one inch thick. The photo shows that this thin slice of Tenino sandstone could be suspended in midair without breaking. Shown in the photo (left to right) are H. P. Scheel, William McArthur, __ Jonis, John Jonis, Andrew McArthur and Isadore Jonis. (Author's Collection.)

Flat cars loaded with rubble stone destined for the Grays Harbor jetty await the switch engine at Hercules Quarry No. 2 north and east of Tenino after the Big Blast of February, 1912. (Author's Collection.)

Huge boulder was blown onto the railroad track at Hercules Sandstone Co. Quarry No. 2 north of Tenino by the Big Blast of February, 1912. (Author's Collection)

The crew of Hercules Sandstone Quarry No. 6 in the Skookumchuck Valley posed for the camera in 1915. (Author's Collection)

Steam-powered crane, mounted on flat car, was used to load rubble stone on flat cars at Hercules Sandstone Quarry No. 6 in the Skookumchuck Valley, about 1915. A. D. (Punch) McArthur is shown at controls. (Author's Collection)

Main office of the Hercules Sandstone Co, 1912. Shown (l-r), H. P. Scheel, ____ Johnson, bookkeeper, William McArthur. This building is now a part of the Tenino city hall. Note the sandstone wall panels. (Author's Collection)

Andrew Wilson, star stonecutter of the Hercules Sandstone Co., about 1909. (Marenakos Rock Center Collection)

Indian Louie Quityamals and his daughter, 1892. (South Thurston County Historical Society Collection)

Tenino and Its Industries. This photo was used as a part of a promotional brochure published by the S. H. Fink Co. of Olympia about 1904. It contained a number of photo illustrations of the Tenino area. The only known remaining copy of the brochure is in the Archives of the University of Washington. (Author's Collection)

Blumauer Lumber Co. saw mill, Tenino, 1909. (University of Washington, Special Collections, Neg. No. UWA. Curtis 15091)

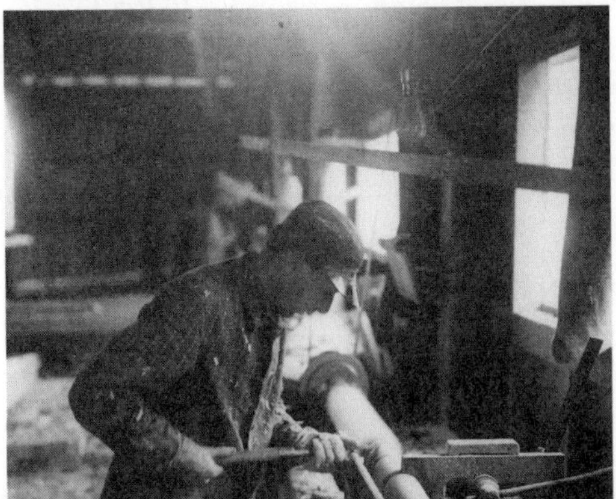

Interior of Blumauer Lumber Co. saw mill, Tenino, 1909. (University of Washington, Special Collections, Neg. No. A. Curtis 15095)

Student body and faculty of the Tenino Public School posed in front of the schoolhouse about 1908. This huge wooden schoolhouse was demolished after the new Tenino Grade School was built in the 1930s. (Author's collection.)

The new Tenino Grade School, under construction, 1930s. This school, and its predecessor shown in the background, were on the block now occupied by the Parkside School. (Lyman Smith Collection)

Wood-burning locomotive, with baggage car and one passenger car behind it, blew smoke and steam for the camera at the Tenino depot, about 1885. (University of Washington Special Collections, Neg. No. UW23984)

Ezra Meeker, Washington pioneer, made two world-famous trips over the Oregon Trail, the last in 1910-1913, when he was in his 80s. During that trip he stopped in Tenino and drew a huge crowd to welcome him. At the left, T. F. Mentzer. (University of Washington Special Collections, Neg. No.UW 23985)

The Hans P. Scheel family, at their home in Tacoma. Standing (l-r), Walter, Karl, Lorenz (Larry), Hans, Dorothy; Seated. Frances, Louise, H. P., Margaret and Frances. (Author's Collection)

Guests at the William McArthur family posed before the Christmas tree for the photographer, about 1908. Back row (l-r): William Mullany, Andrew McArthur, Jessie McArthur, Margaret McArthur, Williaml McArthur, Billy Stevenson (?), Robert McArthur. Middle row (l-r): Jim McArthur, Ted McArthur, Willaim D. McArthur, Bill McArthur (Andrew's son). Robert R. McArthur, Carrie McArthur, Bernice (Bunny) McArthur. (Author's Collection)

The Tenino Cornet Band posed for the camera, date not recorded. (South Thurston County Museum Collection.)

The Tenino Eagles Lodge Band played in the park at Centralia, 1920. Standing (l-r): Hans Scheel, William D. McArthur, Frank Wood, James D. McArthur, Lee Lewis, Al Sommerville, Drum Major Dr. ____ Davis, Clarence Caughlin, Tom Slusser, Tom Nelson, ___ Carlson, Willis Rambo, Harold Myers, Tony Frare, Kneeling (l-r): Robert R. McArthur, Gene ____, A. D. McArthur, Ben Meyers, Band Director Robert B. McArthur, Charles Blue, ____ Brown, Earl Davis. (Author's Collection.)

William McArthur, about 1912. (Author's Collection)

HANS P. SCHEEL, about 1930 (David Scheel Collection)

S. W. (WES) FENTON, date not recorded. (South Thurston County Museum Collection)

Robert R. McArthur, 1921 (Author's Collection)

A group of locals (possibly the Board of Directors; William McArthur is fourth from the left) gathered in front of the State Bank of Tenino building, about 1912. Note the board sidewalk. (South Thurston County Museum Collection.)

Tenino's leaders gathered for a stag event in the woods near Offut Lake, about 1912-13. Left to right: Andrew McArthur, Harry Richards (lumberman), William McArthur, T. J. McClellan, S. W. Fenton, Jim Stephenson, H. P. Scheel and Isadore Jonis. The record does not indicate what was being passed in this picture. (Author's Collection)

William McArthur (left), his brother, Robert McArthur, and William McArthur's patented retort for making illuminating gas out of Tenino coal. Note the row of lighted gas jets to the left of the photo. (Author's Collection)

Hercules Sandstone Co. crew posed in one of the "coyote holes" deep in Quarry No. 2. Andrew McArthur is at the left. These tunnels were packed with dynamite and black powder which was exploded February 17, 1912, breaking up stone to be used in the Grays Harbor jetty. Note in foreground the rails over which tiny handcars were rolled to pack in the 44,600 pounds of explosives used. (South Thurston County Museum Collection.)

Tenino honored its returning World War I veterans with a parade down Sussex Avenue on Flag Day, 1919. The band led, returned service men came next and behind them were the white-clad mothers and Red Cross civilian volunteers. (Author's Collection)

Tenino decorated its cars and joined the Tenino victory celebration parade on Flag Day, 1919. (Author's Collection)

After the grand Victory Parade on Flag Day, 1919, Tenino's returned World War I veterans were honored in a banquet at the Francis Hotel. *(Author's Collection)*

The crew of the Beaver Lumber Co. sawmill at Tenino, about 1919. *(Author's Collection)*

Members of the Southwestern Washington Development Association visited Hercules Quarry No. 2 in April, 1913. Seated at left is Hans P. Scheel. (Author's Collection)

Sussex Avenue, Tenino's main street, looking east from Ritter Street, about 1917. (University of Washington Special Collections. Neg. No. 23986)

Eighth grade graduation class, Tenino Grade School, 1914. Top row, left-right: Miss Uddenberg, teacher, Dorothy Angel, Myrtle Schultz, Carrie McArthur, Thelma Tope, Pearl Thomas, Louise Gorline, Edna Keithahn, Marie Mullaney, Adeline Wherrett; front row, Wendell Mawson, William McArthur, Fred Jones, James Sadow, William T. Mullaney, Maurice Cole, Emmett Snyder, Robert R. McArthur. (Author's collection)

T. F. MENTZER, about 1920. (South Thurston County Museum Collection)

13

DISEASE AND HEALTH CARE

Disease was a continuing threat. By the turn of the century, most folks had the opportunity to be inoculated against smallpox. But other diseases came and went.

Medical science didn't have much to offer other than quarantining those who were ill in hopes that would keep it from spreading to others.

Not too many years after the McArthur family moved back to Tenino, the family came down with measles. Grandma and all four kids were stricken ill. William McArthur didn't catch it. The house was ordered quarantined. William McArthur had the quarry to operate, so he left his wife and the kids at home and moved to the hotel until the quarantine was lifted.

Under standards of the time, this was not considered a callous act of disregard.

Later on, there was a diphtheria epidemic. Uncle Andrew McArthur's family was stricken ill but Uncle Andrew was not. The family was quarantined and Uncle Andrew stayed in the hotel until the quarantine was lifted.

Today, people in the United States drink tap water without the least concern. Public water supplies around the start of the 20th

Century often were the source of disease. In December 1913, 17 persons died and 288 others were made ill with typhoid fever at Centralia. Baffled local health officials called on Dr. Calvin S. White of Portland, secretary of the Oregon State Board of Health, to find the cause. Dr. White blamed the town's water supply. All but six of those stricken got water from the local system, which pumped its water from shallow wells at the edge of the Skookumchuck River. That river, Dr. White said, "reeks with pollution."

The problem was not unique to Washington. At about the same time Salem, Oregon had similar problems with typhoid fever attributed to polluted water infiltrating the water system from the Willamette River, which also served as a dumping off point for upstream sewer systems

Contemporary accounts indicate no serious typhoid fever problem in Tenino.

Later, Tenino had a resident dentist, but in the early years it did not. Art Dwelley in his book tells of Wilson Howe, who came to Tenino in 1889 and worked at the Tenino Sandstone Co. quarry. Howe somehow had obtained a pair of dental forceps. Using a toolbox as a chair, Howe would pull the tooth while William McArthur's brother, Andrew (Tim) McArthur, then working as a blacksmith at the quarry, held the patient's head.

There were are least two dentists who visited Tenino periodically from Olympia. One was Dr. Burns. He drove to Tenino and parked his car on the main street. People who needed a tooth pulled would stop—no appointment needed. He would pull the tooth right on the street. Dad said he tossed the extracted tooth into the gutter.

Another dentist set up a dental chair and foot-powered drill in the drug store. He would drill out the tooth and put in a filling while the public walked by outside and came in to make their purchases.

While the McArthur family was in eastern British Columbia, death struck the family's oldest child. Ruby Beattie McArthur was 2 years old in March 1898 when she was stricken with the croup. The McArthurs were living in Salmo. William McArthur was working in the silver mine at Ymir, about 7 miles to the north. He stayed in Ymir during the week and came home only on weekends.

In 1959 my Dad, Robert McArthur, visited Salmo, B. C. and found Sarah Grutchfield, the midwife who had delivered him 59 years before. She was an early friend of the family. Sarah Grutchfield told him that William McArthur arrived home one night to find Ruby critically ill. There was no doctor in Salmo. The nearest medical help was in Ymir. There was no public transportation, no one in the town had an automobile in those days and a blizzard was blowing. Bundling up his wife and the baby, William McArthur and one of his friends took a railroad handcar from the siding at Salmo and started pumping it by hand up the track to Ymir. Ruby died in the midst of the blizzard before they got there.

Those who got really sick or were seriously injured in early 20th Century Tenino were taken to the hospital in Centralia. Tenino didn't have an ambulance. But there was an ambulance in Centralia. It came and got the patient and took him to the hospital.

In October 1923 one of the locals got married and his friends organized a charivari for him at Offut Lake. Two cars were racing on the way back to Tenino and Dad's cousin Bob McArthur was a passenger in one of them, a new Maxwell touring car. The car turned over at Lycan's Corner at the north edge of town (now the intersection of the Tenino-Olympia highway and the road to Rainier). Bob was fatally injured. His brother, Andrew (Punch)

McArthur was in the car, too, as was L. E. Newman. Both were badly hurt.

Dad's brother Bill was there and went to Uncle Andrew's house. That's Andrew McArthur, father of the injured young men. Bill woke Uncle Andrew up and told his that "Cousin Bob" had been hurt bad and that they'd sent to Centralia for the ambulance. Dad's folks were out of town and Andrew McArthur thought it was my Dad that Bill was talking about. He went down to the Lycan house where they had laid Cousin Bob out. Uncle Andrew rode in the back of the ambulance to Centralia. It wasn't until they got him to hospital that Uncle Andrew discovered that it was his son Bob and not my Dad who was injured.

Washington's workers' compensation program paid only death and disability benefits.

A group of local employers, headed by Isaac Blumauer of the Tenino's Blumauer Lumber Company, bought the Centralia hospital for $21,000 and set up shop to treat injured workmen. There was a premium of $1 per month per employee, paid either by the worker or by his employer. The hospital then treated workers injured on the job free of further charge. Benefits ended when the injured workman was discharged from the hospital.

That came in handy for Ed Betts, an employee of the Hercules Quarry No. 6 up the Skookumchuck River.

Dad worked there as a timekeeper the summer of 1915. His cousin, Andrew D. (Punch) McArthur, was operating one of the three big booms used to load the rock onto flat cars. The friction block that acted as a brake on the block slipped. The boom fell across the derrick and pinned Ed Betts beneath it. Dad said he was there when they lifted the boom and slid it off him. At first they thought Betts was dead. They had no telephone in the camp, so Dad's cousin Bill (Hen) McArthur, who worked at the quarry as a blacksmith's helper, ran six miles down the track to the Billy Lewis farm, which was located at the end of the county road and had a telephone. Hen McArthur called Centralia for the ambulance. The quarry crew loaded Betts on a handcar and took him to the end of the county road where the ambulance picked him up and took him to the hospital at Centralia. Betts was badly injured but he did survive.

The Spanish flu came to Tenino as elsewhere in the nation in the fall of 1918. A quarantine was imposed on the whole town. School was closed. Services at the Methodist church were suspended and the Lotus Theater, Tenino's movie house, closed down.

Influenza was not the only epidemic to sweep Tenino in 1918. The Tenino school was closed in March of that year because of an outbreak of measles. Tenino News editor P. C. Kibbe criticized the decision to close the school and commented that the kids were going to catch the measles whether they attended school or not.

In 1920, there were still fears of the Spanish Flu epidemic. William McArthur and his old quarry partner Hans P. Scheel plunged into the realm of alternative medicine. No patent was issued but it appears that their so-called "Inhalatorium" likely was the product of the inventive genius of William McArthur.

Built in a small building next to the Francis Hotel, it featured several telephone booth-sized compartments in which sufferers, who had stripped down to their skivvies, sat and breathed "electro-medicated vapors", which essentially were the smoke of burning local subbituminous coal.

Advertisements in the Tenino News proudly declared the Inhalatorium offered "a New Scientific Method to Aid and give Speedy Relief" to those afflicted with asthma, catarrh, boils, tumors, goiter, rheumatism and skin diseases. The ad didn't say anything about black lung disease.

At its opening, the editor of the News declared the new Inhalatorium brought would-be patients from Centralia, Chehalis, Tono and the surrounding country and found the treatment a relief for those afflicted with the flu. Treatments cost $1.

The ads ran from February through August of 1920 and then disappeared from the paper. Hans Scheel's granddaughter, Sally Phillips, wrote the memoirs of her mother and other Scheel children. They said for a while the booths were full as was the waiting room.

14

LIQUOR IN TENINO

Before Prohibition Tenino had as many as 11 saloons. For a lot of unmarried men who worked in the mills, woods and quarries the saloon was their social life.

Prohibition came to Washington State January 1, 1916.(1) The last night before Prohibition became the law much of the town was drunk. The rest of the folks in town stayed home and pulled down their window shades.

The next morning Tenino was quiet as the hangovers wore off. For a while, the provident lived off the pre-Prohibition booze they had saved. Then the bootleggers started making the stuff up in the Bald Hills. A quart of 150-proof bootleg cost $3. For a year or so the law-abiding could get a permit from the county assessor and import from another state, where sales were legal, up to two quarts of hard liquor and 12 quarts of beer every 20 days. Few did.

Some of the folks were death on liquor. Margaret McArthur

---

(1) Tenino almost went dry in 1912. A petition to put a local option prohibition measure on the November 1912 election ballot was thrown out by the Thurston County Superior Court which held that its backers failed to turn in enough signatures. It took signatures equal to 30 per cent of the votes in the most recent town election.

wouldn't allow the stuff in the house. William McArthur enjoyed a drink. He kept his bottle in the pump house. The pump house was built in the days before Tenino had a water system. In those day each house had a well. The McArthurs had a pump and a raised tank in a tower. This allowed the luxury of running water.

The McArthurs liked to entertain. When guests were at hand, periodically during the evening William McArthur would announce to the men: "Gentlemen, it is time to grease the drum." They would all file out the back door to the pump house and their libation.

In those days a drunk was a drunk, not a candidate for social reform. As long as he didn't harm someone else, no one really cared what he did to himself. William McArthur's brother, Robert McArthur, was unmarried and the best blacksmith in town. Sadly, Uncle Bob drank to excess. Every six to eight months he would fall off the wagon. He would spend his savings and even sell his shoes to buy liquor.

Uncle Bob worked for William McArthur at the quarry. When Uncle Bob failed to show up for work, William McArthur would fire him and hire another blacksmith. The stone cutters would complain that the new man couldn't keep their tools as sharp as Bob did. Grandpa McArthur would cuss, bail Uncle Bob out of jail, get him on his feet again and put him back to work. Uncle Bob would solemnly promise, "I appreciate this, Billy. I'll never do it again."

But he would.

There are a number of stories within the McArthur family about Uncle Bob and his weakness for the bottle.

Dad told of coming home one night before Prohibition:

"I was so embarrassed. I was walking past the saloon. Uncle Bob was passed out on the sidewalk and the town marshal was trying to put him in the wheelbarrow to take him off to jail."

Edna McArthur was married to Jim McArthur. Jim McArthur was Andrew McArthur's son. Jim operated a grocery store in Tenino for many years. Edna recounted that she and some high school friends were walking up the alley one day and found Uncle Bob passed out on his back in the grass.

"We went home, got a bed sheet, picked a bouquet of flowers, put them in his hands and covered him up with a sheet and left him lying there," she said. "I always wondered what he thought when he woke up."

Tobacco was in common use in Tenino as elsewhere in the nation. Men smoked cigars and pipes. They chewed and spit. A common complaint was that women pedestrians had to lift their skirts while passing certain of the saloons and other gathering spots for the tobacco-chewing males. Some men spit on the sidewalk and women had to lift their skirts to keep from getting them spoiled.

Cigarettes made their common appearance after World War I, but they were reluctantly accepted.

Some – William McArthur among them – tried growing their own tobacco. They had indifferent results. The weather is better for tobacco in the South.

And women, of course, did not smoke. Well, the better among them.

15

HOME TOWN MUSIC

Tenino made its own music.

The Tenino Band started in 1892. But it soon gave up being a band and became a fife and drum corps. One writer said Tenino's first town band only mastered one tune and people got tired of hearing it.

The Tenino Drum Corps had one great performance each year, as the stars of the 4th of July parade and the annual "Battle of Pea Soup." Edith Newell in her memoirs printed in the Independent, listed as members Wes Fenton, Andrew (Tim) McArthur, Will Howe, Jimmie Stevenson, Rich Betts, Ed Betts and Bill Mullaney. Membership was somewhat fluid and musical skills not great.

C. Frank Stone, a stone cutter, organized the Tenino Cornet Band in 1902. The Tenino Cornet Band had uniform jackets and hats and it played in the Fourth of July parade every year. It also went with the Commercial Club which chartered a train to go to South Bend about 1910.

Bob McArthur, Andrew McArthur's son, played first cornet and became the leader of the band in 1908.

Later the Tenino Cornet Band became the Tenino Eagles Band. The band had white duck trousers, white shirts and white hats that it wore in the summer and wool tunics for the winter. The Tenino Eagles band was excellent for a small town. It traveled and played at Fraternal Order of Eagles conventions at Victoria and San Francisco.

Both bands were brass bands. But the Tenino Eagles Band had one clarinet. Mike Ruggeri, the town druggist, played the clarinet. Ruggeri also played the violin. Mike and his wife were married in Seattle. The story was that when he courted her he would stand under her window and play love songs on his violin.

Sometime during this period, a two-story bandstand was built on the north side of Sussex Avenue just east of the hotel. It was taken down sometime in the 1940s.

The Tenino Eagles Band died out before World War II. It was resurrected for the V-J Day victory celebration in August 1945, and again for the 4th of July celebration in 1949.

16

INDIAN LOUIE

Indian Louie Quityamals was Tenino's resident Native American. He and his wife lived in a shack next to Del Axtelle's slaughterhouse at the east edge of Colvin's Prairie. Louie was the watchman and custodian there. He fed the livestock, looked after things and lived on scraps from the slaughterhouse and the charity of the community.

Indian Louie was an old man. They said he was born about 1832. A photo of Louie in the South Thurston County Museum bears the penciled notation on the back that the photo was taken in 1892 when Louie was 56 years of age. That would make his date of birth 1836. Most of the Native Americans in the area were chased off to the reservations in the mid-1800s, but Louie was not.

The story was that Louie, who was supposed to have been a sub-chief of one of the Indian bands native to the region, had sided with the settlers during the Indian wars of the mid-1850s. He reportedly served as a scout with the militia and tipped off the White folks of an impending Indian raid that allowed the defense of the blockhouse near Centralia. That made him the friend of the White Man and an outcast to his blood brothers. In his prime, Louise worked as a farm hand and was reported to be an expert grain cradler.

Indian Louie was sort of the town character. He rode the white mule at the head of the Fourth of July parade every year. You can see him in the picture of the parade that is in this book.

Every holiday William McArthur had a dinner and invited a house full of guests. Regularly Louie would show up at the back door for a handout.

One year William McArthur bought an improved model of the Edison talking machine. The Edison phonograph had a big horn on top of it and played blue cylindrical phonograph records. The improved model not only could play phonograph records, it also had a separate cutting head. You could make your own records on blank, brown wax cylinders. You could even shave the cylinders smooth and use them over again. You recorded your voice by speaking or singing into the horn.

That year Indian Louie showed up at the door and William McArthur invited him in. McArthur and his guests had taken turns speaking into the horn and then hearing their voices come back.

William McArthur wound up the new phonograph and stood the old man in front of the bell. One of the guests. Sarah Colvin Taylor, spoke to old Louie in his native tongue.

"Karmika? (Who are you?)", she asked.

Louie answered: "I am Louie, chief on Scatter Creek." Then he paused. (The pause is important.) The crowd urged Louie to speak further and he did. Louie repeated his name, told what he had done as a boy, who he married and about his children. He talked about their deaths and other events of his life. The recitation went on for about five minutes.

William McArthur rewound the machine, changed to the playing head and then played Louie's recitation back to him.

"I am Louie, chief on Scatter Creek," the machine squawked out. "No!" thundered Louie, alarm on his face. "I am Louie." The machine repeated: "I am Louie." Then the machine went on to parrot what Louie had recorded. Louie was quite overcome. William McArthur and the other guests attempted to explain the technology of the recording machine. Louie would not understand. He gathered up his coat and left. He never again came back to the McArthur house and never again asked for a handout there. "You have a devil in your house," he would declare. "No one else knows about my family and I will not go where there is a devil."

I heard that recording about 1942. Dad's brother, Ted McArthur, had the machine in his basement in Olympia. The machine and the records later were stolen in a burglary.

17

THE TOWN'S BARBERS

Men didn't shave that often in the days before World War I. If you shaved yourself, you did it with a straight-edge razor. That was quite a chore. Dad said he shaved with a straight-edge razor until safety razors became popular about World War I. The first safety razors had a single-edge blade. Gem was considered the best.

There were always at least three barber shops in Tenino in those days. Barbers came and went. Norm Clowers was the most successful barber in town. He came to Tenino in 1893 from Missouri and cut hair in Tenino for more than 50 years. Clowers originally worked the channeller at the Tenino Stone Co. quarry. He cut hair on the side. Then he opened up his shop full-time.

Among the other barbers were Sim Lewis, C. L. W. Miller and a fellow who came up from Rochester. His name was Shorty. Shorty was so short that he had built a horseshoe-shaped platform around the back of the chair. He'd stand on the box while he cut your hair. C. L. W. Miller lived on what now is McArthur Street across the alley from the William McArthur house. His wife used to have one of the McArthur kids take Lewis' lunch down to the shop for him on Saturday. She paid the kids a nickel for doing that. Sim Lewis had his shop next to the Tenino Theater. He cut hair in the front. There was a pool hall in the back.

Barbers didn't take Mondays off in those days. They worked 8 a.m. to 6 p.m. six days a week. On Saturdays they stayed open until they ran out of customers. Sometimes Clowers would stay open to 11 o'clock at night.

Haircuts cost 35 cents. A shave was 15 cents.

Norm Clowers also had a bathtub in a room off his barber shop. He sold baths as well. The hot water came from coils in the coal stove in the shop. Clowers' shop was next to Rogers' Saloon. The saloon became a feed store after Prohibition. Clowers charged 25 cents for the bath.

The bath tub was used a lot. Many unmarried men didn't live have bathing facilities where they lived. Loggers would come to town on Saturday night and take a bath in the old-fashioned tub. When one had finished it was his job to wash out the tub and leave it clean for the next guy.

Many of the players who came from out of town for the baseball games would use the tub after the game.

Clowers also had a pool table in the barber shop for those who were waiting. He didn't charge the kids anything for using the pool game, even if they weren't waiting for a haircut. Dad said he played a lot of pool there.

Norm Clowers had two chairs in the shop. When things got busy he had a high school kid in to help him. Norm would cut the hair and do the shaving. The kid would shave around the neck and lather up the shave customers for Norm. That was before you had to have a license to be a barber.

Wiliam McArthur always got shaved by a barber. Twice a week. That's about as often as any man got shaved. The barbers cut with scissors and comb and used hand clippers for shaping. They used several different hair lotions. Fitch was a popular one. The barbers used bay rum afterward as a shaving lotion.

The barber sometimes would give you a massage after the shave. He charged extra for that. He'd steam up your face by piling hot towels on your face, leaving just a little room for your nose so you could breath. Then he'd put some kind of astringent paste on your face to clean out the pores. He would squeeze out the blackheads and put alcohol on your face. Dad said it felt good.

18
THE TOWN'S LAWYERS

There were two lawyers who served a number of years in Tenino, P. C. Kibbe and T. F. Mentzer.

Kibbe came to Tenino in 1904. Kibbe was considered the brightest and best of Tenino lawyers. But he wasn't a talker. Some folks called him "Punkin Head" because his head was shaped like a pumpkin. Kibbe was involved in oil and gas development in the area. He was a poet, and he also published the Tenino News for about five years.

T. F. Mentzer and his brother, C. A. Mentzer, owned the Mentzer Brothers mill north of town. Mentzer bought the mill from Frank Bard in 1889. It produced both lumber and shingles. The Mentzers also had a mill in Tacoma. Then T. F. sold his mill and opened a law office in Tenino. His wife and the rest of the family lived in Tacoma. T. F. lived in the back of his law office and went home on weekends.

Mentzer had served in the South Dakota Legislature in 1887 and was in the Washington State Legislature in 1892.

Mentzer also owned other business properties in Tenino. In 1927 he helped organize the short-lived Tenino Canning Co.

T. F. Mentzer was elected mayor of Tenino in 1908. He was

quite an orator. T. F. had served in the Union army during the Civil War. The kids liked to see him invited to speak at assemblies at the school. He made patriotic speeches. He'd get carried away and start swearing and that really tickled the kids.

T. F. Mentzer was a nervous man, too. Old timers told of the time that he was pedaling down the road on his bicycle. T. F. spotted a rock in the road. He shouted, "I am going to hit that God-damned rock. I know I'm going to hit that God-damned rock." He did, and he took a spill. T. F. was so worried about hitting the rock he forgot to steer around it.

Three other Tenino lawyers were Jeff Cannon, Ben Sawyer, in Tenino from about 1908 to 1910, and H. D. King, from 1912 to 1914.

19

THE COMING OF THE AUTOMOBILE

The first automobile came to Tenino in 1905. It was a Brush, a now long-defunct auto. It belonged to Dave Copping. He had a hardware store next to the Masonic Temple. Copping later was mayor. The Coppings lived across the alley from the William McArthurs. Dave Copping came home one night and drove through the end of the garage. The neighbors guessed he couldn't stop it.

The first place in Tenino that sold gasoline was Leslie J. Johnson's garage. Johnson had started his business in 1903 as a shoe shop. Then in 1904 it became a bicycle shop. It later became an automobile garage. At one time Johnson was the local dealer for Overland automobiles.

There were a half-dozen different automobile dealers in Tenino through the 1920s. The truly successful operation was that of L. E. Titus, a Ford dealer headquartered in Olympia. Dad worked for Titus for a number of years and was sales manager when the company went broke in 1932. In the 1920s the Tenino newspaper carried advertisements for four other local automobile dealers. They were L. J. Johnson, Overland; Penny's Garage, Star; Yantis & Hall, Studebaker, and C. C. Stearns, Gray Truck. William McArthur bought a 30 horsepower EMF touring car in 1913. It was a 1912 model. William McArthur got his gas from the same distributor that Johnson did -- Western Petroleum Co. of Centralia.

Western Petroleum delivered gas to the McArthurs and to Johnson, too. It came in a wagon drawn by two horses. Johnson had a barrel for gasoline in the back of his garage. The oil wagon driver would carry gasoline from the wagon in 5-gallon cans and dump it in Johnson's barrel. When you wanted some gasoline someone would go out back and fill a bucket from the tap and carry it out to the car and pour it into the tank through a funnel made from a 5-gallon can with a spout welded to the top.[1]

William McArthur kept his barrel of gasoline in the garage where he kept the car. This was on the corner of the highway where Harry Penney later had his garage. Dad and his brother Bill always gassed up Grandpa's car. They would take the gas out of the barrel and dump it in the tank under the front seat of the car. Then they were allowed to start up the car and drive it to the house for Grandpa. That was their reward. They got to drive the car to the house.

Thomas Finan, who had an insurance agency in the back of Norm Clowers' barber shop, bought a new car about 1916 or 1917. He decided he was going to go to Olympia and buy a new Dodge. But Finan didn't know how to drive. So he took Dad along. Dad knew how to drive.

They went to Olympia and Thomas Finan bought the car. The salesman told Finan he'd teach him how to drive. The salesman took them out in the car and showed Finan how to steer, and how to stop and shift the gears. Then, while the car was still going, he shouted, "Just keep her going and you'll do all right." And he jumped off the running board and hoofed it back to the garage. Dad and Finan got home all right.

20

POLITICS - TENINO STYLE

Folks in Tenino liked to argue about politics. Norm Clowers' reminiscences in the Thurston County Independent told of the frequent fist fights that took place between supporters of S. W. (Wes) Fenton and T. F. Mentzer, rival candidates for the 1894 state legislature.[(1)]

Tenino was incorporated and its first government formed in 1906. Henry J. Keithan, who had come to Tenino in 1898, was its first mayor. Now that there was a town council, this gave folks even more to argue about.

Tenino's town government always was a low-budget operation. Initially, Tenino financed its municipal operations with a $500 annual tax on saloons (there were six of them at the time) and $3 a day license fee on vendors of "medicines, drugs and nostrums."

Local politics was not particularly democratic. Dad said that William McArthur and some of the acknowledged leaders of the

---

[(1)] Fenton won that election with the support of Indian Louie Quityamals, Tenino's favorite Native American. Until well into the 20th Century, state law prohibited Indians from voting in Washington elections. But Wes Fenton supporters figured Louie ought to have the vote. Louie did, and told the election board he wanted to vote the "Pippen" (Republican) ticket.

town would get together before each election to decide who ought to run for the town council. That was in the days before the Australian, or secret, ballot. Voting was called "vive voce". That meant the voter stood in front of the election judges and anyone who wanted to watch. The voter told the election judges how he wanted to vote and they wrote it down. This did have an advantage. If a man—women didn't vote then—promised you his vote, you could tell whether he delivered or not.

One of the more unusual political efforts of the time was the effort in May and June of 1914 to move the county seat from Olympia to Tenino.

William McArthur and Joe Taylor championed the effort.

The Thurston County courthouse in downtown Olympia was getting crowded and there were rumblings about building a new one.

Tenino, its enthusiasts claimed, would give free land and provide building materials – local stone and lumber – at cost. The new courthouse, they claimed, could be built twice the size of the existing one. And, they said, it wouldn't cost the taxpayers a nickel. Property values were so high in Olympia that the price of the new building at Tenino could be met from selling the old one at Olympia.

And—ahem—Tenino had each day 14 main line passenger trains through its limits. Olympia had none.

Petitions were circulated in Tenino, Bucoda and Tono. Then the effort fizzled out.

The William McArthurs, on a couple of occasions, had the governor as a guest for Sunday dinner. He came down from Olympia by train. After dinner the governor and William McArthur went into the living room, closed the sliding pocket doors that cut it off from the rest of the house, and talked politics. Grandma and the kids stayed in the kitchen.

William McArthur, like most of the businessmen of his time, was a staunch Republican. In 1914 he was a member of the Thurston County Republican Central Committee.

In September 1914, the local Democratic party was in free-fall. Some of its enthusiasts hooked up with the remnants of Theodore Roosevelt's Progressive Party. They called themselves the Fusionist Party and met at Olympia to nominate a slate of candidates for local office.

William McArthur, they thought, would make a fine county sheriff. They nominated him for the job.

But they forgot to ask him first if we wanted to be the sheriff, and more important whether he was willing to run for the office as a Fusionist.

The day after the news came out, William McArthur rejected the nomination. In a letter to George Yantis, secretary of the Fusionist convention, McArthur declared:

"I am a Republican in all the name implies, believing that the party is better fitted for the management of the affairs of this government."

He was not the only nominee to reject the dubious honor offered by the Fusionists. Frances Sylvester refused nomination as county school superintendent. She was a Socialist.

William McArthur's political views were inherited by most of the family. I was a kid in junior high school in Tacoma in 1945 when Franklin Roosevelt died. My Dad came home from work that night and I breathlessly asked him: "Dad, did you hear that President Roosevelt died?" "Yes," he replied. "And no matter how you feel about it, don't say anything. There are a lot of Democrats in this neighborhood."

21
CRIME IN TENINO

There were two homicides of record in the Tenino area in the early 1900s.

In January 1914 M. C. Cole, former saloon keeper, shot and killed Dr. C. E. Ronson, then took his own life. Newspaper accounts said Cole had suffered from "a diseased brain."

In November 1912, Nellie Hinds, resident of the upper Skookumchuck Valley, shot and killed her husband, Herman Hinds. The couple was in the midst of a divorce. Hinds was shot as he broke down the back door of the family home. Nellie Hinds had a restraining order barring him from the home. She pleaded self-defense. The jury agreed.

The local bank was alert to the possibility of robbery. As a part of its own crime-prevention program, the bank passed out rifles to the business establishments at each end of town. They had one at the Titus Garage. The rifle was kept loaded. If there was a bank robbery in town, the citizens were supposed to shoot the robbers as they fled the town. It must have worked. There was never a bank robbery.

Tenino's jail was in the town hall. This was about a block north of the present town hall and on the opposite side of Sussex Avenue.

It was a two-cell affair in a wooden building.

It also wasn't much of a jail. That was proven by John Paul Nickrenz, also known as John Paul Nickernz, John Paul McKenzie and John Doe.

Nickrenz was a burglar. He broke into Mayor Howard Barclay's dry goods store. Several days later Nickrenz was arrested by police in Portland as he attempted to hock the merchandise taken from Barkley's store.

Ever a man of quick action, Barclay, who like others of political prominence in Thurston County had been commissioned a special deputy sheriff, promptly went to Portland, a pair of handcuffs in hand.

Barclay brought Nickrenz back to Tenino and lodged him overnight in Tenino's jail. An hour later Nickrenz was discovered to have pried loose the screen over the jail window and made his escape.

Several days later Nickrenz was again arrested in Portland. This time he was returned to the county jail at Olympia, where he confessed and was promptly sentenced to one year in prison.

Before he could be transferred to state custody, Nickrenz again broke jail. He pried open the lock on his cell door and fled the untended county jail.

However, he left behind a note explaining why he decided not to stay:

"Dear Sirs:—I hate to do this but I am nearly prostrated from nervousness from solitary confinement. Am nearly worried to death. Please don't pursue or I will be tempted to do away with myself."

Nickrenz was pursued, and he didn't do away with himself. He went back to Portland where he was again recaptured. This time he stayed in jail until he pleaded guilty to second degree burglary and jail breaking. He was sentenced to 18 months in Monroe State Reformatory.

Tenino had a policeman. For a while it was a man named Hughes. Another one was Jim Case. When a fellow got drunk and passed out on the street, Jim Case would load him onto a wheelbarrow and haul him off to jail.

Dad insisted that those who had been arrested from being drunk and causing trouble were put out to work on the city streets and roads with a ball and chain attached to their leg.

After World War II Tenino bought a police car. The first one was used part of the time as the driver training car for the high school. Andrew (Punch) McArthur was the policeman.

Tenino became known as a suspected speed trap. One of the recipients of a speeding ticket in 1947 was the driver for U. S. Senator and presidential candidate Robert Taft.

This was not the only time that speeders in Tenino made the news. In May 1913, Mrs. George A. Mottman, wife of Olympia's mayor, learned of the illness of a family member in California. She missed to south-bound Shasta Limited and hired a driver and a powerful Winton Six motor car to try to catch up with the train at Centralia. The driver, Lynn Brown, rocketed through Tenino in his successful effort to catch the train.

The Morning Olympian reported:

"The newly elected justice of the peace (not identified by name) however, in keeping with the proverbial country justice, soaking 'them rich city fellers,' had a warrant issued. The fine was the maximum, $50 … "

When the I-5 freeway was opened, and north-south traffic no longer coursed through Tenino, traffic court fines dropped markedly. In 1953 they were $6,885, in 1954 they were $4,676, and in 1955 they were only $987.

22

FIRE AND THE FIRE DEPARTMENT

Tenino had three big fires, in 1905, 1906 and 1917.

The 1905 fire started in George Sumption's grocery store at the corner of Sussex Avenue and Olympia Street. It burned all the buildings in that block except the saloon on the opposite corner. Arson was suspected.

In 1908 fire destroyed buildings on the south side of Sussex Avenue and west of Howard Street and also a building across the street.

In November 1917 fire burned the Masonic Hall, the three-story Central Hotel building and the hotel and barber shop buildings between them.

These fires effectively destroyed most of Tenino's wooden commercial buildings and led to the construction of the stone- and brick-front buildings that still distinguish downtown Tenino.

The big fire of 1905, which was futilely fought with a bucket brigade, gave impetus to Tenino's incorporation as a town in 1906. One of the first things the new mayor, Henry J. Keithan, did was to appoint Leslie J. Johnson as the fire chief. This was well before Tenino finally organized its fire department in 1909. Johnson was fire chief from 1906 through 1945.

The 1905 fire also stimulated the start of a private water company. The town council gave a water system franchise to S. W. Fenton in 1907 and he began construction of water system that would deliver water under pressure to fire hydrants. His franchise required that the water system have a 500,000-gallon reservoir with a water level 140 feet above the second step of the Tenino State Bank building then under construction. The reservoir was built atop Lemon Hill west of town.

The fire department had two big-wheeled hose carts in the town hall. That's where the fire bell was located, also. When there was a fire, someone would run to the fire hall, ring the bell and then whoever was handy would come in his car, hook a hose cart to the back bumper and drive off to the fire. Volunteer firemen would then hook up the hose to a hydrant and squirt. There wasn't much pressure, but it was better than a bucket brigade.

Tenino bought its first fire truck, a used 1924 model, from Renton in 1928 for $750.

Fire was not exclusive to Tenino. On August 12, 1920, fire destroyed the entire business district of Bucoda.

23
WORLD WAR I

The coming of World War I changed Tenino as it did all of America.

Tenino should have known that it was coming. John E. Zenner's weekly Tenino News was filled with accounts of the war in Europe. The News was a tabloid-sized newspaper of four pages. The front page was filled most of the time with boilerplate national news. Except for truly outstanding events, local news was relegated to page 3.

Britain entered the war in August 1914. S. W. (Wes) Fenton, one of Tenino's prominent citizens, was in Ontario, Canada, his place of birth where he was visiting family.

His friends worried that Fenton might not be able to get back across the U. S.-Canada border. So they drew up an "official" Tenino, Washington passport and took it around town so all the downtown regulars could sign it.

All that it lacked to look really official was an official seal. The Town of Tenino didn't have one.

So they affixed prescription bottle labels from every drug store in Tenino, paid the extra postage for international mail, and shipped it off to Fenton at his temporary Canada address.

Fenton did get back to Tenino OK. History is silent as to whether he ever presented his "official" Tenino passport to the border agents.

The war did boost the price of rubber automobile tires. The most popular Goodyear tires increased in price from $18.40 to $22.10.

America entered the war on April 6, 1917. On June 5, 1917, registration was held for the draft. All over America every young man aged 18 to 30 was ordered to sign up for the draft. Registrars for Tenino were George Sumption and F. L. Stokes. In Tenino, 153 young men signed up.

Immediately upon America's entry into the war, a Home Guard company was organized in Tenino. A separate Home Guard unit was organized at Tono.

L. H. Hubbard, cashier of the Citizens Bank, headed Tenino's Home Guard company. The Home Guard had no uniforms and was armed with wooden drill rifles. But it drilled twice a week, participated in the raising of the new 24 x 40-foot American flag at the Mutual Lumber Co. mill and marched with the Tenino Fife and Drum Corps in the Dewey Day parade at Olympia. The Home Guards at Tono sponsored a benefit dance with proceeds going to the local Red Cross auxiliary.

The first draft notices were sent out to Tenino men in mid-summer 1917.

When the second levy was of six men was shipped out in September 1917, the proprietor of George's Place, a cafe, hosted a going-away banquet the night before for the draftees and their friends. T. F. Mentzer, Tenino's premier patriotic speaker, gave the address.

The local Eagles lodge had to elect four new officers to replace men who had either been drafted or enlisted. One of the departing lodge officers was Dr. F. W. Wichman, commissioned as an officer in the Medical Corps and stationed at Camp Lewis.

It didn't take long for some of Tenino's young men to get to the scene of battle in France.

William T. Mullaney, aged 23, enlisted at Camp Lewis, near Tacoma, June 25, 1917. Six weeks later he was in France. By late September he was in action and shortly thereafter was taken ill. Mullaney died at an Army hospital in France of what the Army called "articular dilation" October 22, 1917. Tenino's American Legion Post No. 93, organized at the close of the war, was named after William T. Mullaney. Mullaney was one of five young men from southern Thurston County who lost their lives in military service during the war.

Tenino enthusiastically participated in the various Liberty Bond drives.

But the big Home Front activity was conducted by local chapters of the American Red Cross.

Red Cross women's groups were organized throughout the community. Separate groups were listed for Tenino, Tono, Plumb Station, Lower Skookumchuck, the Altar Society, Order of Eastern Star, Mutual Lumber Co. camp and the Degree of Honor.

The women put together bags of incidentals for shipment to front line units. They stitched together dozens of pajamas and bed spreads for the military hospitals.

The federal government provided skeins of olive drab yarn to women who would knit socks, wristlets and sweaters for the Army troops. Margaret McArthur was one of the knitters. She hiked daily the mile to the farm home of her friend, Frances Scheel, yarn and knitting needles in her bag. There, the two women who had witnessed the rise and fall of the Hercules Sandstone Co. chatted and knitted. H. P. Scheel's daughter, Margaret, says she remembers that Margaret McArthur properly dressed for her hike to the country in a long skirt and high button shoes.

World War I ended November 11, 1918. The Armistice was declared in the early morning hours. There was no radio or television in those days and no one thought to phone or telegraph the news to Tenino.

The town found out the war was over shortly before dawn when Bob Lowery and Jim McArthur came down from Tacoma with the news.

The homemade cannon, normally fired only on the Fourth of July, was primed and fired. Wes Fenton strapped on his bass drum and pounded his way up and down Sussex Avenue. Volunteers rang the fire bell and the bell at the school.

Tenino poured out into the streets. All business was suspended for the day. Logging camps and mills shut down.

The owners of the town motor cars began decorating them and at 3 o'clock in the afternoon a spontaneous parade began. The automobiles were decorated as floats representing America's wartime allies—England, France, Belgium, Italy, Japan, China and Romania.

The town band played. Tenino's war mothers marched in ranks, each carrying a service flag with a star for each member of the family in the service.

This was followed by the celebratory discharge of firearms and all the fireworks that could be found in town. A public dance was held on the street in front of the post office. At midnight, the band played "Home Sweet Home," and the festivities ended.

Robert McArthur and his brother, Bill McArthur, graduated from Tenino High School in June 1918. Their draft notices did not come until after they had enlisted in the Army in October 1918. Both were sent to a student training camp at the University of Washington at Seattle. But the war ended November 11, 1918 and by December of that year both were discharged and sent home. Dad said there were a number of discharged soldiers on the train he rode from Seattle home to Tenino. Many of them were drunk. They were happy that the war had ended.

On Flag Day, June 14, 1919, a grand community celebration marked the end of the war. Tenino's returned service men got back into their uniforms and marched in a victory parade down Sussex Avenue. Also a part of the parade were the area's surviving veterans of the Spanish-American War, Civil War and Indian wars. Afterwards at the city park a citywide barbecue was held, followed by a patriotic speech by Thomas M. Vance, Olympia lawyer. That evening traffic was blocked from Sussex Avenue and a community dance was held on the asphalt in the front of the Tenino post office.

Later, the community treated the returned soldiers and sailors to a banquet at the Francis Hotel, by then managed by William McArthur and H. P. Scheel, who had retreated to the hotel business after the failure of their other ventures.

On November 11, 1919, Tenino veterans marched with others in the Armistice Day parade at Centralia. Members of the radical International Workers of the World razzed the parading veterans and a riot broke out that saw several deaths, including the lynching of a local IWW leader. Dad said that when the fights broke out, one of the older veterans there turned to him and said, "Go home, kid." Dad said he did just that.

24

THE LEADERS

A. – WILLIAM McARTHUR

William McArthur, my grandfather, was born and raised in Bannockburn, Scotland. The McArthurs were laboring men. The genealogy, as far as I have able to trace it, shows quarry workers, coal miners, tartan weavers and one pub keeper. William McArthur learned the quarryman's trade in the stone quarries south of Edinburgh. He emigrated to the United States in 1887, worked for a while in Alabama and came to Tenino in 1889 where he was hired as the foreman in the Tenino Sandstone Co. quarry run by Van Tine and Fenton.

He brought my grandmother, Margaret Goldie Beattie McArthur from Scotland to the U. S. and they were married at Tacoma in 1893. After a hiatus of several years in Salmo, British Columbia, when the quarries in Tenino were closed because of the Depression of 1893, William McArthur and his family returned to Tenino in 1903. There he teamed up with Hans P. Scheel and Claus Clodius to start the Hercules Sandstone Co. That was to be the high point and the disaster of his life.

In addition to his skills as a quarryman, William McArthur was an inventor.

A search of the records of the U. S. Patent Office at Washington, D. C., shows that he owned or had an interest in 10 patents issued between 1909 and 1924.

Most had to do with the coal and oil he knew or thought he knew was beneath the soil of Thurston County. Others were just plain eclectic.

In January 1910 William McArthur and John Weiss, a resident of Chehalis, applied for a patent for an attachment to a horse-drawn street sweeper. Street sweepers in those days were two-wheel carts with a rotary brush that was linked to the cart wheels. As the wheels turned so did the big brush. The patent was for a scoop that was dragged behind—like the grass catcher on a hand-pushed lawn mower—and picked up the debris and horse droppings swept from the street by the sweeper.

Another was a complicated system of electric lights that indicated which seats in a darkened movie theater were unoccupied.

A third was a formula for making floor tile out of a mixture of sodium silicate (waterglass) and volcanic ash. (I always wondered what William McArthur would have done with the surfeit of volcanic ash from the Mt. St. Helens eruption of May 18, 1980.)

His most enthusiastic work—and the only one that made him money—was to figure out another use for the low-grade coal being produced from the mines in the Tenino area. William McArthur made his own illuminating gas. The gas was manufactured from Tenino coal in a sandstone furnace in a shed behind the house. It was piped into the house to a solitary gas lamp.

He further experimented with gas purification, taking over the sunroom where Margaret McArthur, kept her indoor plants.

The experiments killed all the plants.

A byproduct of his experiment was a process for making mineral dyes. He sold that patent for $25,000 to a Chicago man who expanded upon it to break the German cartel on aniline dyes. That money in part financed William McArthur's trip home to Scotland in December of 1913. He went solo and left the family at home. Upon his return the children asked him, "How did you find Scotland?" His laconic answer: "It is small." The rest of the money went into the company.

Although he may have been terse in described his journey to the family, William McArthur was eloquent in describing his travel experience to a reporter from the Morning Olympian, which published a full account in its issue of February 6, 1914.

He described his visit to the obligatory tourist sites in London and New York City. But the Morning Olympian writer waxed eloquent with McArthur's description of New York City nightlife:

"He saw the tango, bunny hug and turkey trot danced and was satisfied in this own mind that they were one and all a disgrace to civilization—at least they were as he saw them."

In June 1915 William McArthur and the Hercules Sandstone Co. announced plans to build an aniline dye plant in Tenino. McArthur said planning would be completed as soon as Quarry No. 6, the granite rubble stone quarry up the Skookumchuck River, was in operation. But the cancellation of the contract for stone from that quarry and the ultimate failure of the Hercules company apparently derailed plans for the dye works.

Another patent was for a locomotive boiler that was designed to use oil and lignite coal interchangeably. His final two patents were for a system to extract oil from oil sands.

The William McArthur family, upon its return to Tenino in 1903, settled into a house at what now is 209 S. Wichman Street. That house still stands. Soon, William and Margaret McArthur bought a larger, two-story house across the street and one block north at 158 Wichman Street. Dad said this second house originally was located at Tenino Junction and was moved back to town when the Tenino Junction development failed. He also said the house previously was a hospital. (There is nothing to substantiate this. The promotional brochure dated about 1904 of the S. H. Fink Co. shows another house, similar to but not the McArthur house, was the Tenino hospital. In those days the hospital usually was a private home that kept patients needing more than out-patient care in their own homes.) This second McArthur home many years later was damaged by fire and most of the second story was destroyed.

In 1912 the McArthurs moved to a house at 698 West Sussex Street. That house still is in the family. It is owned by Lee Ann Mandery, daughter of Bernice McArthur Mandery, who was the daughter of William and Margaret McArthur.

B. – HANS P. SCHEEL

Hans P. Scheel was the brains behind much of Tenino's stone quarry development. A masterful and innovative salesman, he helped build the Hercules Sandstone Co. into a chain of quarries in Western Washington and eastern British Columbia before the company crashed in the months before the start of World War I.

Hans Peter Scheel was born into a stonecutting family in Germany in 1866. He emigrated to the United States with his father, Hans Hinrich Scheel, in 1882. H. P. Scheel moved to Portland, Oregon in 1882 and met his wife, Martha Louisa Christina Franziska (Frances) Stein, in Tacoma in 1889.

H. P. Scheel's nickname was "Horse Power" for his legendary ambition. Among other skills was his talent for computing prices in his mind. Scheel was a partner in the Tacoma stonecutting business of Simpson & Scheel. At the start of the 1893 Depression he moved to Olympia and took a job as a stonecutter at the Fenton & Van Tine quarry in Tenino, staying in Tenino during the week and walking the 15 miles home to Olympia each weekend. It was there he met William McArthur with whom he later would partner in the development of the Tenino area's stone industry.

Scheel moved to Spokane in 1896 and became a partner in what eventually would become the Washington Monumental and Cut Stone Co. The company provided stone for a number of prominent buildings in Eastern Washington.

In 1903, Scheel, Ritzville banker Claus Clodius and William McArthur organized the Hercules Sandstone Co. and opened Quarry No. 1 west of Tenino. Scheel soon sold his Spokane-area holdings to concentrate on the Tenino company.

H. P. Scheel was the moving force and master salesman of the company, which at one time boasted business offices in Tenino, Tacoma, Seattle and Vancouver, B. C. Scheel later became an investor in the Paraffin Oil Co., the Western Coke and Coal Co. of Seattle, the Washington-Oregon Oil Co., Spokane Marble Co., American Onyx and Marble Co., Royal Climar Group Mining Co. of Spokane and the State Bank of Tenino. He and McArthur owned the Francis Hotel in Tenino, renamed by Scheel after his wife. Among the Scheel family's eight children were two sons, Walter and Karl, who were prominent in the business. Another son, Hans Jr. (Heinie), developed stone deposits in northwestern Washington and owned the Scheel Stone Company and Western Mineral Company both of Seattle. The Scheel's youngest son, Lorenz (Larry), was the last of the old-line stone cutters. Among his other works, he cut stone for the Thurston County courthouse in 1930. Larry Scheel died in 1999 at the age of 91.

Scheel, his wife and their eight children lived in a mansion on

Prospect Hill in Tacoma. Frances Scheel had an 8th grade education, but was well-read and trained in both music and culinary arts. She proudly spoke "High" German. The Scheels lived well in Tacoma. The family had a maid, a cook, a gardener, a washerwoman and a steam-heated greenhouse in which the family grew flowers and out-of-season vegetables. H. P. Scheel drove what was claimed to be the first Cadillac automobile on Prospect Hill. H. P. was a meticulous dresser. His suits were custom-tailored, and his shirts had detachable celluloid collars.

All that came to an end when the cancellation of the government jetty project just before the start of World War I drove the Hercules Sandstone Co. into bankruptcy. Scheel had personally guaranteed loans for the opening of Quarry No. 6. When the government contract was cancelled, the loans could not be repaid. Scheel lost all of his holdings except for a tract of farmland at the North edge of Tenino.

The Scheel family lived one year in the barn on the property until they were able to build a house. The family kept house in one half of the hay mow. Hay filled the other half. The livestock was downstairs. Frances Scheel, never looking backwards at the luxurious life the family had known, set about raising her family of eight children on the farm, cooking, washing clothes, burning stumps, weeding the garden, butchering stock and milking the several cows the family kept on the farm. While she worked, Frances Scheel occasionally would burst into song. Much of her repertoire was grand opera. She knew much of Wagner by heart.

H. P. Scheel set about to recover financially.

He later opened a gravel pit north of Tenino and made a modest living. He died at Tenino in 1940.

C. – T. J. McCLELLAN, TENINO'S ENTREPRENEUR

Tenino's leading entrepreneur was T. J. McClellan. He came to Tenino from Kansas in 1890 with his wife and seven children.

McClellan had a hand in just about everything that happened in Tenino except the stone industry.

McClellan owned and operated a sawmill and shingle mill at Tenino and logged the hill west of Tenino. He operated a general mercantile store in 1891. He and a partner started a creamery in the south part of Tenino. McClellan then opened a drug store. In 1905 he built the first telephone system in Tenino. In 1906 he built the town's first electric utility system and later started Tenino's first movie house. Tickets were 10 cents each. McClellan was a charter member of Tenino's Masonic Lodge.

T. J. McClellan was a patriotic man. He was a Union Army veteran. He had fought in the battle of Gettysburg.

Dad said he delighted in telling the youngsters stories about his experiences in the Civil War. The kids asked that he be allowed to come to the school and tell the whole student body about it, but the principal, D. A. Barber, wouldn't let him. Dad said it was rumored that Barber favored the South.

In his declining years, McClellan was Justice of the Peace and Tenino Police Judge.

D. – S. W. (WES) FENTON

Samuel W. (Wes) Fenton was the pioneer quarryman of Tenino, and in person a man bigger than life.

Fenton was born in 1861 in Ontario, Canada, and served his apprenticeship there. At the age of 18 he went to work for Thomas Russell at a salary of $4 a month plus board.

By 1888 he was working in a limestone quarry near West Superior, Wisconsin, helping quarry stones for cross-street arches in St. Paul, Minnesota. It was there that he met George N. Van Tine. Van Tine and Fenton heard of a shortage of building stone in the Pacific Northwest and decided opportunity lay there.

Arriving eventually in Olympia they explored the Manville quarry near Plum Station north of Tenino as a possible source of stone for a minor building boom being experienced in the Seattle area. It was not a good day. Fenton and Van Tine didn't like the quality of the stone. And they missed the last train that would take them from Plumb Station back to Tenino.

They spent the night at the home of a nearby farmer, Sam Spurlock. Spurlock had a fireplace built of sandstone. The stone was blackened by smoke but the two quarrymen scraped a patch clear with a knife and noted the stone was of good grain and quality. Spurlock told them that the stone had been hacked with an axe from sandstone boulders south of Tenino, and that other fireplaces locally had been built in the same manner.

The next morning the would-be entrepreneurs rode the narrow-gauge railroad back to Tenino. En route they visited with the conductor, Fred Brown, Tenino's first merchant. Brown told them where stone deposits had been found in the area.

Van Tine and Fenton located an outcropping near the Southern Pacific railroad track at the south edge of Tenino and leased it from Charles Billings.

This was the Tenino Sandstone Co. quarry, the first quarry in Tenino (see further details at Chapter 2).

Fenton stayed with the quarry though with various partners until the quarry finally closed for good in 1926.

Fenton served as a member of the Washington Legislature and as mayor of Tenino, and perhaps was best known as the pounder of the bass drum that kept time for the Tenino Fife and Drum Corps and helped awake Tenino to the news of the end of World War I.

After the quarry closed he returned to his original work as a brick and stone mason. Fenton died in 1936.

25

THE NEVER-ENDING QUESTION - HOW TENINO GOT ITS NAME

How Tenino got named in 1873 doesn't really belong in a history dealing with what happened in the town in the early 20th century. But you can't have a book about Tenino without visiting the dispute over how Tenino got its name.

In late 1872 the Northern Pacific Railroad halted construction for the winter of its line from Kalama to Tacoma at what now is Tenino. The place where the track ended needed a name and General J. W. Sprague, head of the NP, named it Tenino.

Some folks contend that Sprague got the name from a survey stake, numbered T-9-0 or 10-90 on the original railroad survey. Others say it was the equipment number of the first locomotive used on the line.

In 1935 C. Lee Martin, Tenino's school superintendent, decided to settle for once and all the origin of Tenino's name.

In a series of seven articles printed at the top of page one of the Thurston County Independent December 1935 through February 1936, Martin explored in excruciating detail the issue of the name.

He printed in full a letter from the chief engineer of the Northern Pacific Railroad who said there was no survey station 1090 at

Tenino and, likewise, no locomotive No. 1090 was on the route.

The first assistant Postmaster General wrote that the name of the Coal Bank post office, originally opened April 17, 1860, was renamed Tenino on November 17, 1873. But, he said, there was no record of how the name Tenino was chosen.

Professor Edmund Meany of the University of Washington said "Tenino" is an Indian word meaning "fork." There was a fork in the old Military Road about where Tenino was located. William Ragless, Tenino's earliest settler, said he was told by an aged Indian that "Tenino" in the Indian language meant "stop" and it was at what was to become Tenino that construction of the railroad was halted.

But other experts said the word "Tenino" was unknown in recorded Indian lexicon.

However, before J. W. Sprague gave the new settlement the name, "Tenino" was varyingly applied to an Indian tribe in the mid-Columbia River area, a branch of the Deschutes River in eastern Oregon, a steamboat built at Celilo in 1862, and a street in Portland.

Best bet is that Tenino was named for the Columbia River tribe that had no connection to the Tenino of today.

ABOUT THE AUTHOR

Scott McArthur was born in Olympia, Washington and was raised in Tacoma, Washington. He spent part of his summers as a child in Tenino, Washington, his father's home town.

He is a graduate of the University of Puget Sound, the University of Oregon and Northwestern School of Law of Lewis & Clark College at Portland.

Scott McArthur taught in both the public schools and at the college level. He was a reporter for Radio Station KMO in Tacoma, the Associated Press, Albany (Or.) Democrat-Herald, Salem (Or.) Capital Journal and United Press International. He practiced law at Monmouth, Oregon from 1967 to 2002, and now works part-time as an arbitrator and mediator.

This is his second history book. His first, "Monmouth, Oregon: Saga of a Small American Town," was published in 2004.

ON THE BACK COVER: *Grand Marshal W. Dean Hays, in his top hat and astride a well-curried horse, posed before the start of the Tenino parade, July, 4, 1906. (Author's Collection)*